Karen has done it again! *How t...* *Every Time* is a great book that I .... Karen's easy-to-read style of writing, along with her practical advice and biblical guidance, make this the perfect book for anyone trying to find God's direction. It is absolutely packed with wisdom from cover to cover. Before you make your next big decision, read this book!

—BETH JONES
Pastor, Valley Family Church
Author, Getting a Grip on the Basics series
Kalamazoo, Michigan

It doesn't matter if you're a well-versed Christian or a new convert, Karen's ten keys for finding God's direction are masterpieces that will help you in your personal walk with the Lord and show you how to make the right decision every time. Karen lays out God's plan backed up by Scripture and examples, and she finishes each chapter with a review and challenge to "Now Engage" what you've learned. Read it, engage, and enjoy the life God wants you to have!

—JASON CRABB
GRAMMY Award–winning singer-songwriter
Nashville, Tennessee

Another great book by Karen Jensen Salisbury. It's a must-read for anyone looking for God's direction.

—SANDY SCHEER
Pastor, Guts Church
Tulsa, Oklahoma

I know Karen Jensen Salisbury and the wonderful sources she had for gaining the oh-so-valuable information contained in this book—the Holy Spirit and the teachings of my longtime mentor, Dr. Kenneth E. Hagin. I can personally recommend it to you for its practical application in your life.

—Dr. Billye Brim
Author and speaker
Founder of Billye Brim Ministries
Branson, Missouri

Making life's toughest choices need not be hit or miss. In *How to Make the Right Decision Every Time* Karen Jensen Salisbury walks us through the process using life's greatest manual, the Bible, to show us God's clear-cut plan.

—Babbie Mason
Singer-songwriter, author, and TV talk-show host
Atlanta, Georgia

If you're facing any kind of decision in your life, this book is an excellent guide. Karen combines powerful scriptural and practical insight to help you get there. It's a must-read for every Christian, and I highly recommend it!

—Tim Burt
Associate pastor, Living Word Christian Center
Minneapolis, Minnesota

The worst decision you might make is to not read this book! Karen is a gifted writer who has earned the right to be heard and has plenty of good things to say. In this book she gives you the tools you need to make the right decision every time. I think every Christian should read it!

—Rachel Burchfield
Author, *Miracle Moments*
President, Texas Bible Institute
Katy, Texas

Walking in God's will does not have to be a burden, yet most of us struggle with making the right decisions in our lives. How thrilling it is to know that God has a perfect plan for us and that He is more than willing to share it with us! In this book Karen provides ten practical keys that will lead you to discover His plan for your life. We live in a culture that promotes a "do what's right for you" ideology, but how refreshing it is to read Karen's book and know that God's plan is much bigger than that.

—JANET BOYNES
Author and speaker
Founder, Janet Boynes Ministries
Ft. Worth, Texas

Have you failed at decision making or felt uncertain when trying to make a decision? If so, Karen will tell you why in this book. You will be blessed with her directions on how make the right decisions. You will learn how valuable and important you are, and secrets to help you through your lifetime. I recommend this book. I am glad it is in my library.

—NORMA BIXLER
Founder, Cornerstone TV
Pittsburgh, Pennsylvania

Undoubtedly one of the greatest needs of believers is wisdom in decision making and knowing how to discern the will of God. We live in a day when many are pulled in wrong directions by all kinds of negative influences, and countless others opt for instant gratification and the path of least resistance. People often experience heartbreaking results in life and may not realize that their worst enemy was, in fact, themselves. Karen is a solid minister and an excellent writer, and readers will find solid principles of wisdom, guidance, and direction in these pages. Your life will be enriched as you learn to understand and follow the will of God for your life.

—Tony Cooke
Author and Bible teacher
Founder, Tony Cooke Ministries
Tulsa, Oklahoma

How to Make the Right Decision Every Time is a book that will beautifully reassure you that God hears you, that He has a plan, and that He desires you to walk in that plan. Karen writes, "He leans forward to listen to us when we talk, and He *hears us*. We can have confidence that He'll answer us every time we call on Him or ask for His direction."

The ten keys are written to give both spiritual and practical instruction on how to make the right decision every time. The chapter reviews will help you engage and activate what has been written and mediate on the Word, leading you to live a life that is directed and guided by the Holy Spirit.

—Patsy Cameneti
Author and pastor, RHEMA Family Church
Brisbane, Australia

We all face decisions in our lives, and you need to know that God wants to guide you every step of the way. This book can take you from aimlessness to fearlessness and show you how to make the right decision every time.

—Kate McVeigh
Author and speaker
Founder, Kate McVeigh Ministries
Warren, Michigan

How to
MAKE THE
RIGHT DECISION
EVERY TIME

How to

MAKE THE

RIGHT DECISION

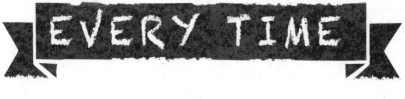

EVERY TIME

KAREN JENSEN SALISBURY

CHARISMA
HOUSE

Some names and stories in this book are composites created by the author from her experiences in ministry. Names and details have been changed, and any similarity between the names and stories of individuals in this book to individuals known to readers is coincidental.

Cover design by Lisa Rae McClure
Design Director: Justin Evans

Visit the author's website at www.karenjensensalisbury.org.

Library of Congress Cataloging-in-Publication Data:

Jensen Salisbury, Karen.
  How to make the right decision every time / by Karen Jensen Salisbury. -- First edition.
      pages cm
  ISBN 978-1-62998-026-3 (trade paper) -- ISBN 978-1-62998-027-0 (e-book)
  1. Decision making--Religious aspects--Christianity. 2. God (Christianity)--Will. I. Title.
  BV4509.5.J46 2015
  248.4--dc23
                                        2014041695

15 16 17 18 19 — 9 8 7 6 5 4 3 2
Printed in the United States of America

To my wonderful husband, Bob Salisbury,
I love being married to you, man of God.
Thank you for coming along and
making the future so bright.

CONTENTS

CAN YOU REALLY MAKE the RIGHT DECISION EVERY TIME?

CASSIE WAS A beautiful girl in her twenties. But as she sat hunched over in the chair across from my desk that day, she was in obvious distress.

"Karen, I don't know what to do or which way to turn," she said, her eyes filled with tears. "I'm so afraid of making the wrong decision. If God would just tell me what to do, I'd do it!"

I've heard statements like those a lot over the years. As a pastor and Bible-school instructor, I've met so many earnest, willing people just like Cassie who want to make the right decisions in their lives, but they just aren't sure how to go about it.

Is that you today? Are you facing a decision in your life—a really big one, or maybe just a small one? Are you wondering which direction you should take? If so, then this book is for you.

We all have decisions to make every single day. Maybe you're wondering if you should move or stay put; get married, stay single, or wait for the real Mr. Right or Mrs. Right; invest a big chunk of money; go back to school; accept a job offer, look for another job, or stick with your current one.

Maybe you're facing a decision about a family member. Or

trying to decide which car or computer to buy. Or whether you want to have children, get a roommate, buy a pet, or take a bold step of faith. Maybe you're just trying to decide what's next in your life. The list is endless. Thousands of decisions are waiting to be made every day.

Whatever you're facing today, I have some good news for you: you *can* make the right decision every time when you have God's help. And even better news is that He *wants* to help you make every single decision—big and small. He knows exactly which direction you should take so that things turn out great for you, and He wants to lead you in making the right decision every time.

There's a Plan

Things started to change for Cassie as soon as I assured her that God wasn't trying to keep her in the dark or hide the answers from her. It made all the difference for her to know that He wanted to help her make the decision she was facing. I explained to her, in fact, that He wanted her to know the right direction even more than *she* wanted to know it, because He had a plan and a purpose for her life that He wanted to unfold.

"I guess I never thought of it that way," Cassie told me. "There is actually a specific plan, and God needs me to be walking in it. Gosh, it makes sense that He would help me find it and not hide it from me!"

The same is true for you—God has a plan and purpose for your life. We often call it, simply, His will for your life. It starts with making you a part of His family. This happens when you accept His Son, Jesus, as your Lord and Savior. Then, as you choose to accept and follow His plan for you, you discover it's a plan that will bless not only you but others too. So He needs for you to be walking in that plan.

We know this is true because the Bible says it is. Jeremiah 29:11 says: "'For I know the plans I have for you,' says the LORD. 'They are plans for good and not for disaster, to give you a future and a hope'" (NLT). The Message Bible says it like this: "I know what I'm doing. I have it all planned out—plans to take care of you, not abandon you, plans to give you the future you hope for."

God's plan for your life will bless
not only you but others too.

First of all, that means there *is* a plan. I'm so thankful for that, aren't you? And it also means that someone knows what the plan is—God knows! I don't know about you, but if I'm facing a decision and don't know which way to go, it comforts me to realize that God knows the plan.

Second, we can see from this verse that it's a *good* plan. God's plan and purpose for you—His will for your life—will lead you into a bright future. When you follow His plan, things will turn out way better than you ever imagined they would—and way better than you ever could have worked out for yourself.

The story of the prodigal son in Luke 15 proves this. It's the story of a young man who asked his father for his inheritance, then went out and spent it all on riotous living. Soon he found himself penniless, feeding someone else's pigs, and barely eking out an existence. One day he thought, "Even my dad's servants eat better than this. I'm going to go home, tell him I've sinned, that I'm no longer worthy to be called his son, and ask him to just let me be one of his servants." (See verses 17–18.)

That was the young man's plan. But when he returned home,

his father didn't stick to the script. The Bible says, "The father said to his servants, 'Bring out the best robe and put it on him, and put a ring on his hand and sandals on his feet. And bring the fatted calf here and kill it, and let us eat and be merry; for this my son was dead and is alive again; he was lost and is found" (Luke 15:22–24).

This is such a perfect picture of your heavenly Father. His plans are way better than yours! He has so much more in store for you than you can even imagine having for yourself. The plans you make for yourself are never as good as the plans God has for you.

So seek and follow *His* plan. It's a plan full of goodness and hope for your life. That's all the more reason to find out *from God* what the plan is, and then turn to Him when making decisions about how to get there.

The plans you make for yourself are never as good as the plans God has for you.

One minister friend of mine says it this way, "Decisions are the doorways to God's plan. If we could see what happens behind the scenes, in the spirit realm, and the future results when God-led decisions are made, we would make it a point always to seek Him and go His way, because His way is always right!"

You're Equipped

When God thinks of His plan for you, He thinks of everything He's done in you and given you that equips you to follow through. You can follow this plan—in fact, you were *made* to follow this plan! And when you do, Jesus says you will walk in the light: "I am the light of the world. He who follows Me shall not walk in darkness, but have the light of life" (John 8:12).

I don't know about you, but that makes me want to walk in His plan and purpose more than anything! It is a wonderful plan beyond your wildest dreams. Why? Because God planned it. And He's been working on it since before you were born. Ephesians 2:10 says, "For we are His workmanship, created in Christ Jesus for good works, which God prepared beforehand so that we would walk in them" (NAS).

Think about it: God *created* you—He handcrafted you—for good works *beforehand*. He set it up for you, and He believes you'll do it. It's your divine destiny. Before you were even born, He prepared these good things for you to do. If you're reading this book today because you're facing some major decisions, that should be good news to you.

Since He created the plan and He created you, doesn't it make sense that He would want to lead you and guide you into it? He's not keeping the plan a secret from you—He wants you to walk in it. He wants to see it all come to pass even more than you do. Life is not a big guessing game, and God hasn't overlooked you. He is standing by, ready to help you make the right decisions so you'll end up walking in your divine purpose.

I think this is where we get off track sometimes. We don't realize there is a divine plan for our lives and that our job is just to find out what it is and walk in it.

Remember when you were a kid in grade school and people would always ask you, "What do you want to be when you grow up?" You probably took all sorts of aptitude tests to find out what you were good at and what career or vocational endeavor you might be suited for.

But wouldn't it make more sense to seek the Creator of the plan, and then follow Him when making our decisions?

Instead of asking, "What do I want to be?", maybe we should be asking, "Lord, what do *You* want me to be?"

I'm telling you—you're here on purpose, just like Cassie. God has crafted you for a specific plan, and He needs you to fulfill it. You need to believe that. And then you need to seek Him about it.

You might pray something like this: "Lord, thank You for leading me into my divine purpose. I will pray and read Your Word and trust You to speak to my heart, letting me know the direction I should go."

Remember, you are the only "you" on the planet, and God needs you in your place! Thankfully He knows the path that you should take. Believe Him to reveal it to you.

He's Paying Attention

Very often when people ask me about making decisions in their lives, I hear them talk as if God isn't paying attention when they pray. I've heard them say things like, "I've been seeking and seeking the Lord, but He just isn't answering." It's almost as if they feel like God has gone on a prolonged vacation and when they call on Him, all they're getting is His voice mail or out-of-office e-mail reply.

In essence these people are wondering, "Is God paying any attention at all to what's going on with me?" They might have read Jeremiah 29:11 and said, "Oh, yes, amen—there's a plan." But they quickly follow that affirmation with, "I don't know what the plan is! God won't tell me!"

They seem to believe God has forgotten about them. Maybe they think He has been distracted by something else and taken His attention off their case.

But I'm here to tell you that nothing could be further from the truth! Matthew 10:30 proves it. It says, "The very hairs on your head are all numbered" (NLT). I think it's one of the most amazing scriptures in the Bible, and it *proves* that God is paying very close attention to the details of our lives.

Think about that. God has counted every hair on your head. Now, I always say that if you're in a relationship with someone who's counting the hairs on your head, then run for your life because that's obsession! But Scripture says God apparently is obsessed with you.

> God is paying very close attention
> to the details of our lives.

But that's not all. For example, almost every morning when I am getting ready for the day, I run a brush through my hair and some hairs fall out. Yet God still knows the number of hairs on my head by the afternoon, which must mean He's keeping a *running count* of the number of hairs on my head.

But it's not just my hairs or yours. Oh, no. He's numbered the hairs on every head *on the planet*. That's right—about seven billion heads!

Now that's a God who's into the details. So don't think for a moment that He's not paying attention to your life and the decisions you're facing. If He knows how many hairs you have on your head, He knows everything else that's going on with you too. You can bank on the fact that He hears you!

Several verses in Psalms paint such a wonderful picture of your heavenly Father and the attention He is paying to you. Psalm 40:1 says, "I waited patiently for the LORD; and He inclined to me, and heard my cry," and Psalm 116:2 says, "Because He has inclined His ear to me...I will call upon Him as long as I live."

You know what I picture when I read that God "inclined to me"? I see Him *leaning forward* from His throne, *inclining* Himself toward me so that He can hear every word, every prayer. The New Living Translation of the Bible says it this way in Psalm 116:2: "Because he bends down to listen, I will pray as long as I have breath!" I love that image of Him *bending down*. That's how closely He is paying attention to you and me.

Then, in the New Testament, we see that 1 John 5:14 says, "This is the confidence that we have in Him, that if we ask anything according to His will, *He hears us*. And if we know that He hears us, whatever we ask, we know that we have the petitions that we have asked of Him" (emphasis added).

How can you have confidence that God is answering your prayers and paying attention to your situation? Because He hears you!

Imagine what it would be like to talk with or pray to a God who wasn't listening, who didn't hear you. That would be a hopeless feeling indeed. There would be no way to believe your prayers were being answered—they wouldn't be! Some people feel that way. They feel as if God is not listening to them or paying any attention to them.

> How can you have confidence that
> God is paying attention to your
> situation? Because He hears you!

But the Bible shows us that isn't true. It says He's numbered the hairs on each of our heads, He leans forward to listen to us when we talk, and He *hears us*. We can have confidence that He'll answer us every time we call on Him or ask for His direction.

Don't worry for a moment—God has you covered. He's standing by, counting your hairs, poised and ready, willing and able to guide you into every right decision for your life.

God Knows the Way

God has always been a guide for His children. It's who He is—it's part of His nature to lead us and help us make the right decisions in our lives. He has set it up so that we would ask Him and He would guide us, because He always has the best plan in store for us. He *wants* you to ask for His guidance, and He wants to guide and direct you—because He knows the way!

We can see this part of His nature in both the Old Testament and the New Testament, where there are countless examples in which God helped His children make the right decisions and go in the right direction. If you're a Christian, then you're His child, and He wants to lead you too.

If you're *not* a Christian, or you're not sure if you are, quickly read "Your Most Important Decision" at the end of this book. You'll learn about the *first* decision you need to make, right now. Without making it, you can't be sure you will make any other decisions correctly, much less make them correctly every time.

Let's look first into the Old Testament to build our faith about how God is a God of guidance—how He wants to direct you and help you make the right decisions in your life.

If you've read through the Old Testament at all or heard some of the stories, then you know that God parted the Red Sea and led His children safely to the other side (Exod. 14). He led them through the wilderness to the Promised Land (Josh. 22:4). He led them in numerous victorious battles over their enemies. He never just left them hanging, struggling to find their own way—even when they were being disobedient and rebellious. He was always right there to lead them if they asked for His guidance and obeyed Him.

Scripture after scripture in the Old Testament shows us how much God wants us to go in the right direction and make the right decisions. In Isaiah 42:16 He says:

> I will bring the blind by a way they did not know; I will lead them in paths they have not known. I will make darkness light before them, and crooked places straight. These things I will do for them, and not forsake them.

When you're trying to make a decision, you're blinded to what the future looks like. You can't see what will happen because you haven't been this way before; you haven't ever taken this path. Your future is shrouded in darkness—you can't see into it yet. You need someone to guide you and light the way, and God is the perfect One to do it.

He won't leave you halfway
through the journey. He'll take
you all the way through.

He says in the verse we just read from Isaiah that He will make the darkness light (no one can do that but Him). When it's light, we can see, can't we? Then He says that where the road bends and you can't see ahead, or when things seem to be so twisted up that there isn't a way to make it through, He'll make those crooked places straight.

He ends the verse by saying He won't forsake you. He won't leave you halfway through the journey. He'll take you all the way through. Believe it!

More Proof

In Psalm 32:8 God says, "I will instruct you and teach you in the way which you should go; I will guide you with My eye." When you have God as your teacher, instructing you, you are in very good shape indeed. He knows everything! We don't know the way, but He does. And He says He'll share it with you—He'll instruct you and teach you which way to go. Isn't that good to know?

He also says He will guide you with His eye. Think for a minute about God's eyes. Do you think they see everything? I do. I think God has seen it all! And when He says He'll guide you with His eye, He means you don't have to be afraid that He'll miss anything. That's because His eyesight—His ability to see the past, present, and future—is perfect.

So you have more than a pretty good guide there!

Can you feel faith rising in your heart when you read these verses? As if God really *can* direct you and help you make the right decision every time? That's what happens when we read His Word—faith comes (Rom. 10:17). I encourage you to *keep reading*—both this book and these verses (out of your own Bible), as well as the "Now Engage" sections at the end of each chapter. You need to keep God's Word in your heart and your mind to keep believing that your heavenly Father can help you make the right decision every time.

Here's more Word to build your faith: "The steps of a good man [or woman] are ordered by the LORD, and He delights in his way" (Ps. 37:23). Your steps take you somewhere, either in the right direction or the wrong direction, and result in your making the right decisions or the wrong ones. But when you seek the Lord and ask Him to direct those steps, they'll go in the right direction every time. And that delights Him, the Scripture says.

Psalm 48:14 says, "For this God is our God for ever and ever: he will be our guide even unto death" (KJV). Mark it: until you die, God will guide you, direct you, and help you make the right decisions. That covers your whole life! You will never face a time when He's not available to guide you.

That means even if you make a mistake or a wrong decision, He'll be there to help you out of it. That should help you if are paralyzed by fear about making a specific decision.

You may be afraid to fail, but you can trust God. He's big enough to rescue you if you goof up. (I'll discuss this more in "Key #8—Get Back on Track.") He said He will always be your guide, even until you die.

> Even if you make a mistake
> or a wrong decision, He'll be
> there to help you out of it.

Even Better

In the New Testament, which is *your* covenant with God through Jesus Christ, God's guidance system for helping you make right decisions gets even better. He promises to lead and guide you by His own Spirit, who lives right inside you:

> When He, the Spirit of truth, has come [which He has],
> He will guide you into all truth; for He will not speak on
> His own authority, but whatever He hears [from God] He
> will speak; and He will tell you things to come.
>
> —JOHN 16:13

The Amplified Bible says it this way:

> But when He, the Spirit of Truth (the Truth-giving Spirit) comes, He will guide you into all the Truth (the whole, full Truth). For He will not speak His own message [on His own authority]; but He will tell whatever He hears [from the Father; He will give the message that has been given to Him], and He will announce and declare to you the things that are to come [that will happen in the future].
>
> —JOHN 16:13

Think about that! The Holy Spirit within you gets directions right from God the Father, who knows everything. Then He passes on that information directly to you. He'll even clue you into what's going to happen in your future. Wow! Information like that can really help you make right decisions, can't it? And you are never without this supernatural help to guide you in making right decisions!

This is why our new covenant, which is bought by the blood of Jesus, is so much better than the old one (Heb. 8:6). In your covenant with God, His very Spirit lives within you. You have the very best guidance system at your disposal, 24/7.

No human can look into the future. But the Spirit of God knows the future—at all times! The Bible says He will tell you about what is coming up. When you know what's coming, you can surely make better decisions, can't you? Romans 8:14 says, "For as many as are led by the Spirit of God, these are sons [and daughters] of God." You could swap that around and say it like this without changing the meaning: "The sons and daughters of God are led by the Spirit of God."

In other words, when you're a child of God—when you are born again and Jesus is your Savior and Lord—you can *expect* to be led by the Spirit of God. In fact, you're not to be led by

13

anything else. That means you can depend on Him to tell you which direction to go when you're trying to make decisions! Start believing that.

⁓⁓⁓⁓⁓⁓⁓⁓⁓⁓⁓⁓⁓⁓⁓⁓⁓⁓⁓

You have the very best guidance
system at your disposal, 24/7.

⁓⁓⁓⁓⁓⁓⁓⁓⁓⁓⁓⁓⁓⁓⁓⁓⁓⁓⁓

In this book we're going to look at ten keys—both practical and spiritual—that will help you make right decisions—the right decision every time! I promise you that by implementing these keys and living by the scriptures they're based on, you'll walk successfully in God's plan for your life and fulfill the destiny He has just *for you*.

REVIEW IN A NUTSHELL

God has a plan for your life, and He wants to guide you in it. It's His very nature to do so. You really can make the right decision every time if you seek and follow Him.

NOW ENGAGE

Read and meditate on the scriptures we've looked at. Activate the power of God's Word in your life by speaking these declarations aloud:

> "For I know the plans I have for you," says the LORD.
> "They are plans for good and not for disaster, to give you
> a future and a hope."
> —JEREMIAH 29:11, NLT

DECLARE: "There is a specific plan for my life, and God knows what it is. He wants me to know it too, and He wants me to walk in it even more than I do. Lord, thank You for leading me into my divine purpose. I will pray and read Your Word and trust You to speak to my heart to let me know the direction I should go."

∽∾∿∽

> For we are His workmanship, created in Christ Jesus for
> good works, which God prepared beforehand that we
> would walk in them.
> —EPHESIANS 2:10

DECLARE: "Before I was born, God had His eye on me, and He handcrafted me to fulfill a divine destiny. I'm going to walk in it. He set it up for me and He believes I can do it, so I'll believe it too!"

The very hairs of your head are all numbered.

—MATTHEW 10:30

DECLARE: "God is paying such close attention to what's going on in my life that He's keeping a running count of all the hairs on my head. He's totally into the details, and He knows everything that's going on with me."

I waited patiently for the LORD; and He inclined to me, and heard my cry.

—PSALM 40:1

Because He has inclined His ear to me...I will call upon Him as long as I live.

—PSALM 116:2

DECLARE: "The Bible says that God is *inclining* Himself toward me. I can imagine Him leaning forward from His throne, bending down to catch every word I say, every prayer I pray. That's how closely He is paying attention to me."

This is the confidence that we have in Him, that if we ask anything according to His will, He hears us. And if we know that He hears us, whatever we ask, we know that we have the petitions that we have asked of Him.

—1 JOHN 5:14

DECLARE: "I have confidence that God is leading me and answering my prayers because *He hears me!* I know He's answering me every time I call on Him or ask for His direction.

He's standing by, poised and ready, willing and able to lead and guide me into every right decision for my life."

∽✐∽

I will bring the blind by a way that they knew not; I will lead them in paths that they have not known: I will make darkness light before them, and crooked things straight. These things will I do unto them, and not forsake them.
—Isaiah 42:16, KJV

DECLARE: "God is the perfect One to lead me in a direction I've never been before because He already knows the way. He is making the darkness light so I can see clearly. He's making the crooked places straight. And He won't leave me halfway through the journey—He'll take me all the way through. I believe it!"

∽✐∽

I will instruct you and teach you in the way you should go; I will guide you with My eye.
—Psalm 32:8

DECLARE: "God knows everything, so with Him teaching and instructing me, I will surely go in the right direction. He will guide me with His eye, which sees everything. I won't miss anything. I have the perfect Guide for this journey."

✑✑✑

> For this God is our God for ever and ever: he will be our
> guide even unto death.
> —PSALM 48:14, KJV

DECLARE: "God will guide me, direct me, and help me make the right decision every day until I die. That covers my whole life! There will never be a time when He's not available to guide me."

✑✑✑

> When He, the Spirit of truth, has come [which He has],
> He will guide you into all truth; for He will not speak on
> His own authority, but whatever He hears [from God] He
> will speak; and He will tell you things to come.
> —JOHN 16:13

DECLARE: "The very Spirit of God lives within me. I have the best guidance system there is at my disposal, 24/7. The Holy Spirit knows the future and can tell me about what is coming up so that I can make the right decisions."

✑✑✑

> For as many as are led by the Spirit of God, these are
> sons [and daughters] of God.
> —ROMANS 8:14

DECLARE: "I am God's child, so I am led by His Spirit. I *expect* to be led by the Spirit of God. He'll tell me which direction to go when I'm trying to make decisions. I believe that!"

DETERMINE TO BE LED BY GOD...AND NOTHING ELSE

WHEN IT COMES to making decisions, big ones or small ones, Key #1 is the most important of all. To make the right decision every time, you must determine in your heart to base it on God's direction and nothing else.

You see, you are in covenant with God, as we read in Hebrews 8:6: "[Jesus] is the one who mediates for us a far better covenant with God, based on better promises" (NLT). When two parties enter into a covenant, it means everything that belongs to one party belongs to the other, and vice versa. In our covenant with Almighty God we like the parts that say His "everything" belongs to us, don't we? Why, our Father owns the cattle on a thousand hills (Ps. 50:10), and that all belongs to us too!

But sometimes we forget the part that says our "everything" belongs to Him. That means we shouldn't make a single decision without asking our covenant partner, God, about the decisions we're facing. He will always lead us in the right direction, but we must determine to let Him lead us and not be directed by anything else.

That might sound like a no-brainer, but we all know that

people make decisions for a lot of other reasons. Let's look at some examples of the wrong things on which to base decisions.

More Money

It's awfully tempting to base a decision on money. It's easy to say, "I know I should take that job because it pays more!" More pay is a good thing, for sure, and God is most certainly not opposed to you having more money.

But acquiring more money shouldn't be your priority in life. God should be your priority. Jesus emphasizes this fact in Matthew 6:33: "Seek *first* the kingdom of God…and all these things shall be added to you" (emphasis added). In other words, seek God first, and He'll make sure you have *everything* you need to live a successful life—more money, yes; but also other things that money can't buy, such as peace, health, and purpose. Money is a poor substitute for following God and being in His plan. Money is a hard taskmaster, and the love of it is "a root of all kinds of evil" (1 Tim. 6:10).

If a certain higher-paying job isn't God's best plan for you, then choosing it based on your desire for more money can set off a chain of events that you don't want to be involved with. You could be miserable at that job. If so, your discontent will lead (at the very least) to stress, which can affect your health. There's just nothing worse than going every day to a job you hate.

And if taking that job means you're not in the place where God wants you to be, then that fact alone will create all sorts of negative consequences, especially if you have a family. Worst of all, if you're in the wrong place, then it means you're not in the *right* place, which means your life is out of order at both ends and you aren't fulfilling your divine destiny.

Lack of Money

Sometimes we let our lack of money make decisions for us. For example, maybe God has been dealing with you to give a certain amount of money to someone or to go on a mission trip. But you haven't obeyed and haven't gone because you don't have enough money. You can't see how you could afford it.

Listen, if God is dealing with you, take a step of faith and believe *Him* for the money. Don't let money decide for you! Where God guides, He provides.

When you seek Him to learn His plan, and then follow His leading, you have *His supply* available to help you make the impossible happen. If He says do it, then it's up to Him to finance it! Your job is to just keep believing Him for it. When you obey Him and step out, His supply becomes available for you in other areas too, such as influence, favor, and ability.

Don't let money decide for you!
Where God guides, He provides.

Maybe God has been dealing with you to do things in a more excellent way, to spend a little more money on things, to not do everything "on the cheap." Being a Christian doesn't mean being cheap or always looking for a handout or a special deal. Our God is a God of excellence and abundance. (I mean, think about it—*His streets are made of gold!*) He wants the same excellence and abundance for His children, especially since we represent Him.

When you're first starting out life as an adult, you don't always have a lot of money. That was true of my first husband, Brent, and I when we were starting out in ministry. We bought cheap things (personally and for our ministry), and then pretty soon we couldn't see ourselves having the best of anything.

One friend of mine really helped me in this area. She and her husband were also starting out in ministry in those days. We all were trying to get hold of the fact that Jesus wanted us to have *abundant* life (John 10:10) and had provided all our needs (Phil. 4:19). We were starting to see those verses fulfilled in our lives, but we still had major areas of "lack thinking" in our minds.

I remember one day when my friend got a revelation of God's abundant provision. God used toilet paper, of all things, to illustrate it to her. (Don't you love how God meets us and teaches us with everyday things?)

She had been using toilet paper just two or three squares at a time to save money. That seemed frugal—it seemed like she was being a good steward of her money. But God spoke to her and said, "Why are you using just three squares? I am your God, and I'm always more than enough!"

Well, when that *rhema* word dropped into her spirit on top of everything else she was learning about God's abundant supply, she grabbed hold of that roll of toilet paper and pulled with all her might! When she was telling me about it, we laughed and laughed together. She told me she declared out loud, "My days of penny-pinching are over! I always have more than enough—even toilet paper!"

Her story helped me for years. Every time I thought about holding back out of fear of not having enough (money or anything else), I pictured her yanking on that toilet paper roll! I would realize I was being fearful and that my God provides more than enough for me when I believe Him.

Now, that doesn't mean we should be wasteful or bad stewards of our money. We should use common sense, be led by

God's Spirit in every area of our spending, and not waste our resources in any way.

But our God is not "El Cheapo"—He is El Shaddai, "the Almighty, the God who is always more than enough!" He isn't wasteful, but He is extravagant. I pray you see the difference and that you never let lack of money hinder you from following His best plan for your life.

The same type of revelation that came to my friend came to me one day when I needed gas for my car. Gas prices had gone up, and people all around me were afraid. Everyone was worrying and complaining about the increase. "Can you believe how high gas prices are!" they'd exclaim. "We can't afford gas at this price! People are going to have to go out and get a second job or cut down on groceries, just to buy gas for their cars!"

Our God is not "El Cheapo"—
He is El Shaddai!

It went on and on. I'm sure you've heard this kind of talk before.

Just as I too had started to panic and wonder how in the world I would survive those high gas prices *on my salary* (I was imagining all sorts of terrible scenarios of lack and fear), I heard these words from the Lord in my heart: "Karen, I'm not at all worried about gas prices. They're never going to get too high for Me. Don't depend on your salary—depend on Me. I am El Shaddai, the God who is always more than enough. In Jesus, I've provided everything you need."

I can tell you, I got the victory over high gas prices that day—and all other high prices too! Now whenever the media and people around me are talking about high gas prices, high grocery prices, high heating prices, and so on, I declare aloud: "Oh, Father, *thank You* that I always have more than enough to pay those prices!"

That is the truth, and I want you to know it today. Say it aloud right now: "Thank You, Lord, that I always have more than enough!"

If we let money make decisions for us, then our choices will almost always be based on either fear or greed. We might be tempted not to fill up with gas or visit that person God has laid on our heart, or to withhold an offering because we see our own financial need coming up, or to say no to something because we're afraid of not having enough money.

> "Thank You, Lord, that I always
> have more than enough!"

God wants you to have an abundant supply, and He wants to provide it. Be sure you're not making decisions based on money.

A Pro-Con List

While it's important to use common sense and investigate all the possibilities, try to avoid making a pro-con list in order to make a decision. When you do, even if it's just in your head, you're relying exclusively on your own natural senses and ideas to lead you. You're trying to figure out your decision (and thus your direction) *on your own*.

Compare this with Proverbs 3:5–6, which says, "Trust *in the Lord* with all your heart, and *lean not on your own under-standing*; in all your ways acknowledge Him, and He shall direct your paths" (emphasis added). I like the way The Message renders those verses: "Listen for GOD's voice in everything you do, everywhere you go; he's the one who will keep you on track. Don't assume that you know it all."

Our human understanding is so limited. But God knows everything. Yes, He gave you a brain and He wants you to use it, but sometimes His direction and the so-called logical direction don't match. Always go with His direction. You don't want to rely only on your understanding because you just don't know everything you need to know.

I remember when I was going to move from Boise, Idaho, back to Tulsa, Oklahoma. I had been pastoring our church in Boise by myself for the four years since my first husband, Brent, died, and I felt like God was saying to me, "Move back to Tulsa." I didn't really want to make the move, but I totally felt like the Lord was prompting me to do it. Now, looking back, I'm so glad I did—there were so many divine connections and dreams-come-true for me and for my sons in Tulsa.

But when I was making the decision whether to move or not, it was hard! I started to make a pro-con list, and it looked something like this:

PRO

- There are good connections in Tulsa.
- God is saying to move there.

CON

- I'm moving farther from my family.
- I'm leaving my church and church family—all our loving support.
- Several people think I shouldn't do it.

- I'm just starting to get the hang of pastoring—church is growing, why quit now?

- It's expensive to move.

- My youngest son is still in high school.

- We are established here. It would be starting over again.

- I love Boise and the Northwest.

- Tulsa is so hot in the summer.

- We've already lived there twice—what if this is wrong?

As you can see, if I had made the decision based only on my pro-con list, the cons would have won, and I never would have moved. That's why it's more important for us to seek God and His direction than to go by our own knowledge of a situation. We just don't know enough in our own natural minds to understand all the ramifications of a decision. Be sure you're basing your decision on what God is saying to you more than anything else.

Don't Let Circumstances Decide

It can also be very tempting to base your decisions on whatever *circumstances* you happen to be facing, instead of looking to God and asking for His guidance. Don't base your decision on the circumstances! They may look a certain way, but they don't tell the whole story. Circumstances look different to God than they do to you. And they are always subject to change.

Second Corinthians 4:18 tells us, "Do not look at the things which are seen, but at the things which are not seen. For the things which are seen are *temporary*" (emphasis added).

I think one of the devil's favorite lies is, "It's always going to be this way—this situation is permanent." That's usually not true at all. Circumstances change all the time. For example, try to remember what your biggest concern was a year ago, even a couple of months ago. It was probably different from your biggest concern today.

> Take comfort in knowing that
> today is not a life sentence.

That's because circumstances change all the time. Take comfort in knowing that today is not a life sentence.

Things won't always be this way. These circumstances are temporary—you don't want to make a decision based on something that's constantly changing.

God never changes, so He is the surest foundation for decision making. "I am the LORD, I do not change," He said in Malachi 3:6, and Hebrews 13:8 says Jesus Christ is the same "yesterday, today, and forever." You can go to His Word and receive answers and direction because His Word doesn't change from one day to the next. Psalm 119:89 says, "Forever, O LORD, Your word is settled in heaven."

It's much better to base your decisions on someone who is solid and never changes than on something that can look or be different by tomorrow. One minister I know says his favorite phrase in the Bible is, "It came to pass." He says, "It didn't come to stay. It came to pass!"

Now, that may be a loose interpretation of Scripture, but the point is well taken. The storms and troubles of life do pass. Those things we think of as permanent are, in reality, temporary. If you'll determine to stand fast in faith, hang on to God through the trouble, and look to Him to help you make decisions, you're going to come out on top.

God can see the future and you can't, so don't let temporary circumstances make decisions for your permanent future. Don't get distracted by the things going on around you—don't let them be your guide. Instead, determine in your heart and mind that you'll act (or react) only when the Spirit of God tells you to.

Let's say, for example, that you're barely earning enough money at your current job to make ends meet. Plus, you just don't get along with a couple of your fellow employees. Those are your circumstances, and because of them you'd like nothing better than to just get out of there! Then, lo and behold, a new job offer comes along with better pay and a great working environment. What should you do?

> Don't let temporary circumstances make
> decisions for your permanent future.

Well, the answer is, you should seek God. You shouldn't let the circumstances decide for you. First of all, God wants the best for you. He can see your future, and He knows how it's going to turn out. You can trust Him. Remember Proverbs 3:5–6, "Trust in the LORD with all your heart, and lean not on your own understanding; in all your ways acknowledge Him, and He shall direct your paths." That means trust *Him*, not your own understanding of your circumstances. Seek *Him* first, and He'll lead you. You want *Him* directing your path through life.

And don't forget, the circumstances at your current job are temporary. At any time you could get a promotion with a pay increase, or those coworkers could leave. I promise you, no matter how great you think the working environment will be at the new job, there are people there too, and there's a good chance you might not like all of them either. The pay might be higher, but you might be miserable there for any number of reasons. My point is, none of these circumstances should be the decision makers for you. Always seek God first, because circumstances change, and they shouldn't have the final say in guiding you.

Wind and Waves

One story in the Bible points out this truth very clearly. One night all of Jesus's disciples were on a boat in the middle of a lake when something quite unusual happened. They could see Jesus coming toward them, walking on the water. The sight scared the disciples so badly that they cried aloud, "It is a ghost!" (Matt. 14:26).

All of them except Peter. For some reason Peter looked at Jesus walking on water and said, "Hey, Lord, if that's really You, tell *me* to come out there and walk on water too!" (See Matthew 14:28.) So Jesus said, "Come." And as soon as Peter had the Lord's word on it, he climbed right out of that boat—and the Bible says he did, indeed, walk on water (v. 29).

Now, it probably would have been better for Peter if the story had ended right there. Walking on water is a pretty spectacular, miraculous thing to do. It takes great faith to get out of a boat and walk toward Jesus on the water. And Peter did it. At that moment he was looking like a man of extraordinary faith and power!

But you and I both know there's more to the story. We know that as Peter walked toward Jesus, the wind started kicking up waves all around and the situation (Peter's circumstances) started looking a bit dicey. Matthew 14:30 says that when Peter saw the wind and waves, he lost sight of Jesus (he let go of the word Jesus had spoken to him) and got scared. Because he was afraid, he started to sink, and then cried out, "Jesus, save me!"

Thank goodness Jesus reached out and grabbed him. But instead of patting Peter on the back for having great faith, walking on water, and making a gallant effort, Jesus said to him, "O you of little faith, why did you doubt?" (Matt. 14:31). Jesus was saying, in effect: "Peter, you were doing really well. You believed the word I said to you and you were doing it. What made you change your mind?"

Well, the answer is obvious, isn't it? The wind and the waves made Peter change his mind. Something he *saw* (his circumstances) took his heart and mind off *the word* of the Lord (what Jesus had said to him), and he faltered. He changed from believing the word of the Lord to believing the circumstances. He took his eyes off Jesus, believed more in the wind and waves (the circumstances around him), and started to sink.

Circumstances shouldn't
decide anything for you!

I think we've all done that. We hear the word of the Lord and start out strong in faith, as Peter did. But along the way we see things that are contrary to our faith, and we start to falter, believing more in what we see than in what God has told us in His Word.

Let me ask you this: if the sea had been smooth like glass without even a breeze ruffling the water, could Peter have walked on it? *No*—you can't walk on water! So how was he able not only to walk on water but also to do it while the wind and waves were kicking up? It was his believing the word Jesus spoke to him that kept Peter on top of the water.

So, then, think about this: what in the world do wind and waves have to do with the ability to walk on water? *Nothing.*

The same is true of your circumstances. They have nothing to do with God's word to you, just as they had nothing to do with Jesus's word to Peter. They have nothing to do with God's plan for your life. They are subject to change and they are subject to what God has told you in His Word. Don't be moved by them. Circumstances shouldn't decide anything for you!

Feelings...Nothing More Than Feelings

When it comes to making decisions, we can't be led by feelings either. Our feelings are too unreliable. They can change from one minute to the next. It's OK to have feelings, of course; we all have them. But we don't want to be making any kind of decision that is a reaction to anger, bitterness, intimidation, or fear. When it comes to making the right decision, we need to make sure we're on a more sturdy foundation than feelings.

There are many stories in the Bible about God's people and His great leaders who "inquired of the Lord." They sought direction in times when their emotions could have overwhelmed them. One such story is about Jehoshaphat, king of Israel. It illustrates what to do when feelings are running amok but a decision must be made based on God's leading and nothing else.

In this story, from 2 Chronicles 20, three powerful kings joined forces against Jehoshaphat. They marched with their massive combined armies toward Israel to attack (and, basically, annihilate) the Israelites. The vast army drastically outnumbered Israel's army, and, naturally speaking, it looked like complete destruction was coming for God's people.

An interesting twist was that it all was happening because Jehoshaphat made a covenant with the evil King Ahab (2 Chron. 18:1), and God wasn't happy about it (2 Chron. 19:2). So Jehoshaphat was out of God's will and, basically, had caused this catastrophe to come upon his people. (If you have ever done anything dumb and, as a result, brought trouble upon yourself, you're going to like this story!)

In 2 Chronicles 20:2 it was reported to Jehoshaphat that this "great multitude is coming against you from beyond the sea." The very next verse says Jehoshaphat was afraid (v. 3). Well, I guess so! He realized what his disobedience caused, and not only was his life in danger but also the lives of all his loyal subjects. Besides fear he probably felt guilt, panic, and any other number of other emotions. His feelings were probably all over the place. Ever been there? I have!

Seek the Lord

But notice what happens. Jehoshaphat didn't let his feelings determine what he did next. He didn't run for his life, although his fear may have tempted him to. He didn't start crying or carrying on or yelling at everyone around him to do something. No, he did what all of us should do when we're faced with trouble or a decision about what to do. The very next words after "Jehoshaphat feared" are, "[He] set himself to seek the LORD" (v. 3).

Jehoshaphat may have been in a tough place, and he may have been the cause of it all, but he didn't let his feelings rule him. In the midst of that hard, scary situation He didn't run from God (which so many people do when they're in trouble or trying to make a decision), and he didn't let his feelings decide anything for him. No, he ran *toward* God. He put his feelings aside and determined to seek the Lord.

Do you know that God has all your answers? He knows exactly what to do in times of trouble. He knows what direction you should take. He is the *first* one you should run to, especially if you're afraid. In the middle of a test or trial don't run from God—run to Him! And ask Him what you should do.

Not only did Jehoshaphat run to God, but because he was the king, he also got everyone in the kingdom praying and fasting to seek the Lord's counsel. There is power in numbers! As they gathered together, Jehoshaphat prayed an amazing prayer of faith that all of us should pray when we're in trouble.

In the middle of a test or trial don't
run from God—run to Him!

Instead of crawling to God on his belly, begging and pleading for help, he started by magnifying the Lord. "O Lord God of our fathers, are You not God in heaven, and do You not rule over all the kingdoms of the nations, and in Your hand is there not power and might, so that no one is able to withstand You?" (v. 6). Jehoshaphat didn't start praying about the problem or his feelings—He started with the greatness of God, to remind both himself and his people that God is greater than any situation they may be in.

Then he reminded God of His covenant with them: "Are You not our God, who drove out the inhabitants of this land before Your people Israel, and gave it to the descendants of Abraham Your friend forever?" (v. 7). Jehoshaphat didn't bring up his own shortcomings or how he had goofed up. He brought up the unbreakable covenant he had with God. We should do the same when we pray!

After he explained their situation to the Lord in prayer,

Jehoshaphat got down to the nitty-gritty: "O our God, will You not judge them? For we have no power against this great multitude that is coming against us; nor do we know what to do, but our eyes are upon You" (v. 12).

I can't tell you how many times in my own life I have prayed that prayer. I've definitely been in places where I felt like I had no power and didn't know what to do! Very often in a place like that, our feelings threaten to overwhelm us. Instead this verse tells us what to do: we must tell it to God and then put our eyes on Him, expecting Him to show up and do something supernatural to rescue us! Having your eyes on God takes your attention off the problem and helps you magnify His greatness.

And that's exactly what happened for Jehoshaphat and crew. The prophet of the Lord spoke up and said to them:

> Thus says the LORD to you: "Do not be afraid nor dismayed because of this great multitude, for the battle is not yours, but God's. Tomorrow go down against them....You will not need to fight in this battle. Position yourselves, stand still and see the salvation of the LORD, who is with you, O Judah and Jerusalem!" Do not fear or be dismayed; tomorrow go out against them, for the LORD is with you.
> —2 CHRONICLES 20:15–17

Wow! Read that again! Then apply it in your situation. The Lord is with you!

Now, the thing to keep in mind is that while He is supernaturally rescuing you, God will always require some kind of corresponding action on your part. In James 2 the Bible lets us know repeatedly that faith without corresponding action is dead (vv. 17, 20, 26)—meaning we will have to get up and *do* something in the "natural" for God to add His "super" to.

That's what happened in the story of Jehoshaphat. Yes, God

instructed them to stand still and see His salvation. Yes, He told them they wouldn't have to fight and that the battle was His, not theirs. But He *didn't* tell them to just sit home on their couches and eat M&Ms while He did all the work. Oh, no—there was a part they had to play, and it really took faith to do it. (Hint: it's going to take faith for you to do your part too!)

> Having your eyes on God takes
> your attention off the problem and
> helps you magnify His greatness.

They had to get up early in the morning, head out to the battlefield, and get face-to-face with that huge army that wanted to destroy them. Talk about scary! And then those who could sing were appointed to lead the way—lead the army—while singing, "Praise the LORD, for His mercy endures forever" (2 Chron. 20:21).

Now, that wasn't exactly a tried-and-true battle plan, was it? I can imagine the singers might have had all sorts of feelings about that plan. They probably were scared—and even felt pretty foolish! But they weren't going by their feelings, and they weren't counting on *their* strength to win the battle. They were counting on the Lord's strength. So they just went forward, magnifying Him.

And then something amazing happened. The Lord caused those three armies to attack one another. By the time Jehoshaphat's gang got there, the battlefield was littered with dead bodies—so many that it took Israel three days to collect the spoil (vv. 22–25). Now that's a great victory!

The moral of the story is, when your feelings are running high, instead of bowing to them, determine instead to seek the

Lord and follow His direction. I've seen people make decisions based on feelings of loneliness or fear or attachment. Maybe you "feel" like you could never live without your extended family around you (or that they couldn't live without you), but if the Lord is telling you to move, then that's the best thing for you. Don't let feelings talk you out of it.

It's so easy to be overwhelmed and make hasty decisions based on how you feel. But don't panic! Do what Jehoshaphat did. Inquire of the Lord and trust Him to lead you safely to victory.

When your feelings are running high,
instead of bowing to them, determine to
seek the Lord and follow His direction.

When the Pressure's On

Right about now you might be thinking, "Karen, you're talking a lot about how *not* to make decisions, but I want to know how to *make* right decisions!" I hear you, and I promise we're almost there. I just want to cover the wrong ways first so you don't fall into any of these faulty decision-making patterns in your life. And our next step is an important one: don't make decisions based on pressure.

One thing I always remind myself in my own life is that pressure very often comes from the devil. God will never pressure us!

One pastor's wife I know said it this way: "The Holy Spirit leads gently from the inside; the devil drives you." So if you feel like you're being driven to make a decision, stop right there! Make it a point never to make a decision just because the pressure is on. It's very likely to be the wrong decision. Why?

Because it's very difficult to hear God's voice and direction when you're tense and under pressure.

A perfect example of this is when you're buying a car (or stereo or furniture or any other big-ticket item). No offense to any salesmen reading this (because you're great at what you do), but salesmen are usually experts at putting pressure on customers to buy. They'll say things like, "It's on sale today only—if you don't buy right now, you'll miss the great deal," or, "I can't guarantee it'll still be here if you wait until tomorrow." They know if they let you go without buying *right now*, you may not come back, and they will lose the sale.

Anytime you get that "It has to be *right now!*" feeling, stop and take a moment to be aware of what's happening. Ask yourself, "Does it *really* have to be right now?" And ask the Lord, "Father, should I wait on this?"

Obviously there will be times when things need to be done right away, such as during emergency situations. But in my own life I tend to back away from pressure just on general principle, even if the pressure is on me to take advantage of a deal on that car or stereo system or furniture piece I want. It's not the last great deal that will ever come across my path.

I will not make a decision in the midst of pressure! I've learned that it's better to wait until I feel God's peace about something than to jump in because it has to be done *right now.*

I've known people who have felt like the Lord was telling them to move, and they put pressure on themselves with an imaginary deadline. For example, say their apartment lease is up next month. They think, "I have to know by the end of next month whether to make this move or not!" But that's not true. God's timetable is usually not our timetable. He's well able to figure out your housing, so don't get into a hurry; don't get under pressure.

When it comes to making the right decision, the devil loves to put pressure on you. He'll bring thoughts like, "This is your only chance. If you make the wrong decision here, it's over for you!" You have to remember, he's a liar. Jesus said the devil "does not stand in the truth because there is no truth in him. Whenever he speaks a lie, he speaks from his own nature; he is a liar and the father of lies" (John 8:44, NAS).

> Pressure very often comes from the
> devil. God will never pressure us!

So it's a big fat lie that this is your only chance. For one thing, God is the God of second chances (and third chances, and twelfth chances, and forty-fifth chances). And for another, it is not the last blessing that will ever be available to you—any more than it's the last great car deal, stereo deal, or furniture deal you'll get.

Demands From People

There are all sorts of ways the devil loves to pressure us. Very often it can come from other people, from their demands or opinions. It's especially hard when people close to you are trying to pressure you into making a certain decision. They may think they know what's best for you, but the only one who *always* knows what's best for you is God.

You don't always know the intentions other people have when they're trying to push you toward a decision. They may have your best interests in mind, but they also may have their own agendas, or they may just like to control other people's lives.

Your heavenly Father, however, is not a control freak, and the only intentions He has toward you are *good.* He only wants the best for you—His only agenda is for your benefit. You can trust Him when it comes to helping you make decisions—He will only lead you in the right direction.

The Bible records many times when Jesus Himself was pressured by people. Religious leaders of His day tried to pressure Him into showing them who He was. They said, "Teacher, we want to see a sign from You" (Matt. 12:37). I can imagine that Jesus must have been more than a little tempted to show them! Wouldn't you, if you were the King of kings? Wouldn't you want to prove yourself or defend God and just perform some great miracle in front of their unbelieving eyes?

But Jesus didn't succumb to the pressure they tried to put on Him. He was interested in following only one Person: His Father. He didn't fall for their manipulative tests or allow them to pressure Him. Instead He answered them by saying, "An evil and adulterous generation seeks after a sign, and no sign will be given to it except the sign of the prophet Jonah" (v. 39). Basically, He just brushed them off.

Jesus didn't succumb to pressure from people, and we shouldn't either. He simply followed the leading of the Holy Spirit. That's all we have to do, too.

Being a People-Pleaser

I have one friend who admitted to me that she often has let people pressure her when it comes to making decisions. She has always felt the need to please everyone. "It's the one thing I struggle with over and over again," she told me. "Always having to analyze whether I'm making a decision because it's what I feel led to do, or because it's what someone else thinks I should do."

To her, it seems like many people just always know what to do—they're able to move forward without ever looking back.

Meanwhile she has wrestled with trying to please everyone—or discern the voice of God from the many voices around her. Maybe that's you too, and you can identify with how she has felt.

But recently she told me something encouraging. "I'm finally starting to see how second-guessing is so damaging to my faith," she said. "When you waver like that, taking everyone else's thoughts and opinions into consideration, you are never convinced you heard God correctly. But faith never goes backward! It keeps moving forward despite external controversy or conflict."

Jesus didn't succumb to pressure from
people, and we shouldn't either.

We can't live our lives to make other people happy, of course. If we choose to base our decisions on God's leading alone, it will work out best for us *and* for everyone else. You simply do not want to be pressured into a decision based on what someone else thinks.

So we've seen a lot of wrong things on which we can base our decisions. The only way to make the right decision every time in life is to seek God for His direction. We must let *His* say be the final say and not allow ourselves to be distracted or paralyzed by any of the outside forces we've looked at.

So how do you get God's direction? We'll discuss that in the next chapter.

REVIEW IN A NUTSHELL

To make the right decision every time, we need to determine that we'll base our decisions on how God leads us and not let things like money, a pro-con list, circumstances, feelings, or pressure be the determining factors.

NOW ENGAGE

Read and meditate on the scriptures we've looked at. Activate the power of God's Word in your life by speaking these declarations aloud:

> Seek first the kingdom of God...and all these things shall be added to you.
> —MATTHEW 6:33

DECLARE: "I will be careful not to base decisions on money or let money be my priority in life. Rather, I will make God my priority. I will seek God first because He has provided everything I need to live a successful life, such as money and other things money can't buy, such as peace, health, and purpose."

∽∾∽

> God shall supply all your need according to His riches in glory by Christ Jesus.
> —PHILIPPIANS 4:19

DECLARE: "I will not be fearful and base any decision on lack of money. My God always provides more than enough for me when I believe Him. I'll be a good steward of my money, but I won't be cheap. I'll be led by God's Spirit in every area of my spending. God is not 'El Cheapo'—He is El Shaddai, 'the Almighty, the God who is always more than enough!'"

Forever, O LORD, Your word is settled in heaven.
—PSALM 119:89

DECLARE: "My circumstances are temporary, so I won't make a decision based on something that's constantly changing. God never changes. I will base my decisions on what He says by His Spirit and by His Word, rather than something that could look different tomorrow. I won't let circumstances decide for me."

Immediately Jesus stretched out His hand and caught him, and said to him, "O you of little faith, why did you doubt?
—MATTHEW 14:31

DECLARE: "I won't let my circumstances take my heart and mind off the Word of the Lord. I won't take my eyes off Jesus—I'll stay strong in faith, believing Him more than I believe the trouble around me, which has nothing to do with God's plan for my life. Circumstances won't decide anything for me!"

O LORD God of our fathers, are You not God in heaven, and do You not rule over all the kingdoms of the nations, and in Your hand is there not power and might, so that no one is able to withstand You....We have no power against this great multitude that is coming against us; nor do we know what to do, but our eyes are upon You.
—2 CHRONICLES 20:6

DECLARE: "When I'm in a tough place, even if I caused it myself, I won't base any decisions on my feelings of fear or guilt or anger or helplessness. When I feel powerless and don't know what to do, I will put my feelings aside and look to the Lord, just as Jehoshaphat did. God has my answers, and He will tell me what to do."

❧

But He answered and said to them, "An evil and adulterous generation seeks after a sign, and no sign will be given to it except the sign of the prophet Jonah."
—JOHN 11:44

DECLARE: "Jesus didn't succumb to pressure from people, and I won't either. I will follow only the leading of the Holy Spirit."

LEARN to RECOGNIZE HIS VOICE

I KNOW THAT A lot of Christians get frustrated about this subject of hearing God's voice. I can remember when I was a young Christian and older ministers would say, "The Lord told me this" or "The Lord told me that," and I would think, "What do you mean, 'The Lord told you'? Did He just talk to you? Did you hear Him out loud? How did you know it was the Lord?"

I would get more than a little irritated with them. But I have since come to learn, after walking with the Lord for a while, that He is the still, small voice that speaks inside my spirit— and He *wants* to speak to me and guide me even more than I want Him to. He wants to do the same for you. I can tell you that it takes a little practice, but now I hear Him all the time, and He leads me on a daily, even hourly, basis. He wants to do the same for you.

The Guide on the Inside

By "practice" I mean that you get into the habit of asking and listening, being aware of His presence in you. When you're on the job, driving your car, walking into a new situation, helping someone, or even heading to a social engagement, give ear to the Holy Spirit. Say, "Lord, what shall I do in this situation?" or "Lord, which way should I go?" Start by practicing with small things, like finding something you've misplaced or asking which way to turn while driving, and pretty soon you'll get good at distinguishing His voice.

How can you continue learning to recognize God's voice when you're making decisions? The answer is, look to the *inside*—to God's Holy Spirit within you. The Holy Spirit is "The Guide on the Inside," and every born-again believer has Him living within.

> The Holy Spirit is everything we need
> to receive and follow God's direction.

As we discussed in the introduction, the children of God (that means you) are led by the Spirit of God (Rom. 8:14). When Jesus left the earth and went to heaven, He left us His Spirit (a.k.a. the Holy Spirit, or the Spirit of God) to live in us and guide us. The very Spirit of the Lord Jesus Christ dwells in you as a born-again believer: "You know Him, for He dwells with you and will be in you" (John 14:17). Jesus didn't leave us here helpless! He left us with a Helper to assist and support us, and to empower us to finish His work on Earth.

John 14:16 in the Amplified Bible calls the Holy Spirit our Comforter, Counselor, Helper, Intercessor, Advocate, Strengthener, and Standby. He is everything we need to receive and follow God's direction when making decisions in life. We shouldn't look for anything else, or anyone else, to lead us.

Our goal when making decisions should be to recognize

and follow the voice of the Holy Spirit. And we can! John 10:27 says, "My sheep hear My voice, and I know them, and they follow Me." If you have received Jesus as your Savior, then you are one of His "sheep" and this verse is for you!

Because Jesus is talking about you in that verse, read it again—but this time imagine Him saying it like this: "*You* hear My voice, and I know you, and you follow Me." Never forget that! He knows you and *you hear His voice.* And because you do, you can follow His leading. I am not making this up! The Bible says it; therefore it's true.

The Good Shepherd

Jesus is painting a word picture for us in John 10:27. He is the Shepherd, and you and I are His sheep. Of all the things that Jesus was when He walked this earth—healer, Savior, King of kings, Son of God—He only ever called Himself the "good shepherd" (v. 11).

Now, the job of being a shepherd is a humble calling. It's not glorious. Shepherds are outside with the sheep almost nonstop, in every season and every kind of weather. They lead their sheep to food and water (Ps. 23:2–3), they lead them to safe places to sleep, they pull burrs out of their coats, and they rescue them when they fall or get lost. Shepherds are even known to sleep outside with the sheep, and I'm also sure they smell like sheep! There's nothing glamorous about being a shepherd.

Yet that's how Jesus sees Himself in relation to you and me. He doesn't exalt Himself or lift Himself above us. He doesn't demand that we bow down to Him. Instead He reaches out to embrace us and care for us. In John 10:11 He said, "I am the good shepherd. The good shepherd gives His life for the sheep." He has given His life for you, just like any good shepherd who lives to protect, guide, care for, and give his life for his sheep.

He not only died for you and bore your sin, but it's clear from this verse that He also speaks to you—and you hear Him! The sheep learn to recognize their shepherd's voice because a good shepherd is always with his sheep, leading, helping, and guiding them. There could be ten other shepherds around, but when the sheep hear the voice of their own shepherd, they recognize it. Each sheep knows whom to follow. It's no different with you when Jesus speaks.

You Hear Him and Know Him

In my own life, when I saw that Jesus said, "My sheep hear my voice," I started *believing* that I could hear His voice. And if you can hear a voice, you can follow it, right? If a friend of yours calls out to you from across a dark room, "Come this way!", and you hear his or her voice, you can follow the sound until you find your way out. It's the same with hearing the Lord's voice, and the Bible says that *you do hear it.*

So you might as well start saying, "I hear His voice and I follow Him." You might as well get into agreement with God's Word. (We'll talk more about that in Key #3—Watch Your Mouth.)

It's time to start believing the
intent of God's heart toward you
is always good and that you do
know Him and hear His voice.

Too many times I hear Christians saying things like, "I can't hear the voice of God," or "I don't know if God is talking to me or not." But that's not what the Bible says. It says we *do* hear His voice! It also says we know Him. Jesus Himself said, "I will pray the Father, and He will give you another Helper, that He may abide with you forever—the Spirit of truth, whom the world cannot receive, because it neither sees Him nor knows Him; but *you know Him*, for He dwells with you and will be in you" (John 14:16–17, emphasis added).

You know Him! When you know someone, you recognize his voice and you know the intent of his heart. It's time to start believing the intent of God's heart toward you is always good and that you do know Him and hear His voice.

Then you need to listen. By that I mean stop and spend time in God's presence—reading His Word and praying—so He is free to speak to your heart and lead you. Too many times we're so wrapped up in our busy lives that we give God no place to talk with us.

You're probably familiar with the story of Moses and the burning bush in Exodus 3. I think it really illustrates this point of stopping and listening to God.

One day when Moses was just going about his daily business, tending his father-in-law's sheep on the back side of the desert, he noticed a bush that was burning with fire—but not being consumed by it. Curious, he said, "I will now turn aside and see this great sight, why the bush does not burn" (Exod. 3:3).

The very next verse says: "So when the LORD saw that he turned aside to look, God called to him from the midst of the bush and said, 'Moses, Moses!'" (v. 4). That began the encounter between God and Moses when God called Moses to go back to Egypt and demand that Pharaoh release Israel from slavery. But what I want you to notice is that God didn't start talking to Moses *until He saw that Moses turned aside to look.*

In other words, God didn't communicate with Moses until Moses stopped and took the time to listen. It makes me wonder how often God's Holy Spirit may be ready to talk with *us,* but we don't take the time to turn aside and listen to Him. The Holy Spirit is a gentleman. He's not going to force Himself upon you, or even interrupt your everyday life, unless you give Him permission to. Very often, I think, He's waiting for us to turn aside from all our busyness and seek Him. Hearing Him is really more up to us than it is to Him.

I encourage you, especially when you're facing a decision, to spend more time with the Lord. By that I mean spend more time reading the Bible, meditating, listening, and praying. Some of us have a pretty good daily devotional habit. If you don't, you need to establish one. Read the Bible every day!

For many of us, maybe in the morning, we read our one-page devotional and accompanying scripture, then review our prayer list and pray for five minutes. And that's good. But when you're facing bigger decisions, that might not be enough. Sometimes drastic times call for drastic measures. You might need to put a little more time in if you need to hear the voice of God clearly before you can make your decision.

Instead of reading two or three scriptures, read an entire chapter. Or find verses that pertain to what you're believing for, and spend time reading them and mediating on them to soak your spirit in God's Word until faith comes. (See Romans 10:17.) Also, you can use the "Now Engage" sections at the end of each chapter of this book to do just that.

Then spend a little more time praying in the Spirit. (We'll talk about that more in Key #6—Tap Into the Power.) And be sure you spend time just *listening.* So many times when we're in need, we do all the talking during prayer. But prayer is *two-way* conversation between you and God—and He's the one who knows everything! You already know what you know. Instead, you want to know what *He* knows. So take time to listen.

How Do You Know It's God?

I don't know about you, but I've met many Christians who claim God told them to do something, but the end result of their decision turns out really badly! That tends to make us all nervous because we think, "How then do we know when it's God's voice that's leading us?" When we get a leading from God, we might second-guess it and think, "Is that just me? Is it the devil? Or is it really God?"

<hr />

The way to be sure you're
hearing the Holy Spirit's voice
is to spend time learning it.

<hr />

Jesus addressed this question in John 10:4–5. He said about shepherds: "When he brings out his own sheep, he goes before them; and the sheep follow him, for they know his voice. Yet they will *by no means follow a stranger*, but will flee from him, for they do not know the voice of strangers" [emphasis added]. Jesus Himself says you will follow Him and that you won't follow the voice of a stranger—and that includes the devil!

The way to be sure you're hearing the voice of the Holy Spirit, God's voice, is to spend time learning it. How did you get to where you could recognize the voice of your parent, your sweetheart, or your children? You spent time with them. If you were never around them, you wouldn't recognize their voices. Well, it's the same with recognizing God's voice. You get familiar with His voice by spending time with Him, and you do that by reading and meditating on His Word because *that is Him talking with you.*

The Bible is not just a book like other books. It's alive. That's why you can read it over and over—it will meet your need right where you are *today*. Once is never enough! Yesterday's faith is not enough for today's challenge. It's able to give you discernment in spiritual things. The Book of Hebrews says it like this:

> For the word of God is living and powerful, and sharper than any two-edged sword, piercing even to the division of soul and spirit, and of joints and marrow, and is a discerner of the thoughts and intents of the heart.
> —HEBREWS 4:12

Jesus Himself is the Word, in the flesh (John 1:1, 14). So when you're reading the Bible, you're experiencing God's life and familiarizing yourself with all He is and all He has for you. The Bible is your covenant, and like any legal document, you want to get familiar with it so you know what belongs to you. And when you get familiar with the way He talks to you (by reading His Word), you can then recognize a foreign voice, or the wrong voice. When you're well versed in the real thing, you can easily recognize a counterfeit.

<hr>

You and I will never be able to
recognize the real-deal voice of God
unless we spend time in His Word.

<hr>

I once heard a perfect example of this. The way the Department of the Treasury trains its agents to recognize counterfeit US money is by having them spend a lot of time studying *real money*. They get so familiar with the real thing by handling it, looking at it, smelling it, and running it through various tests that a counterfeit bill will jump right out at them because it doesn't react or feel like a real bill.

It's the same for you. If you become so familiar with God

through His Word—by studying it and recognizing how He thinks, acts, and views you—then when a different voice tries to lead you, you'll recognize it instantly as a counterfeit, or a lie.

You and I will never be able to recognize the real-deal voice of God unless we spend time in His Word. That's good news, because it means you are totally in charge of that part! You can decide for yourself how much time you spend in God's Word. Just know that as you do, you'll get more and more familiar with His voice.

The Inward Witness

The main way you and I "hear" the voice of God is not audibly. It's through what I'll call the "inward witness." The Spirit of God will give you promptings in your own spirit, or your inner man (Eph. 3:16), which is the part of you that has been born again and made a new creature in Christ (2 Cor. 5:17).

Promptings are inclinations, or thoughts. I like to describe a prompting as a "knowing in your knower." It comes as you're reading the Word, seeking God in prayer, or listening carefully for His guidance. You'll either begin to feel a peace as you consider the decision or an uneasiness. My spiritual father used to describe the peace as "a smooth, velvety feeling" in your spirit and the uneasiness as a "scratchy" feeling. I think that's a good way to describe it. One way or the other, it's a prompting that comes as you seek God.

Second Corinthians 4:16 clearly shows that you and I have both an "inward" and an "outward" man: "Though our outward man perish, yet the inward man is renewed day by day." As Christians, we are to look *inside* for guidance—to the inward man, the born-again part of us made in the image of God—not to the outward man or to what our physical senses tell us. Nowhere in the New Testament (our covenant) do we find that God will lead us by our physical senses.

In fact, the Bible compares our inward man to a light—something that can illuminate the way. "The spirit of man is the lamp [or the light] of the LORD, searching all the inner depths of his heart" (Prov. 20:27). In other words, our spirit is where light is shone on something, or how we are enlightened. We need to be more aware of our inward man and pay attention to those promptings. That's the inward witness.

I have been led by the inward witness more times that I can count, in big things *and* in small ones. I will often say out loud, "Holy Spirit, which way should I go?" or "What should I do here?" And then I listen—not for an audible voice, but for that "still, small voice" on the inside, in my spirit (1 Kings 19:12–13). I listen for His prompting.

I also do this very often when I am counseling someone. As she sits across from me and tells me her problem, I listen to her, but silently I ask the Holy Spirit: "How do I help this person? What should I say? What's the answer here?" In essence, I have my spiritual antenna up, giving attention to the inward witness that will give me answers about how to best help the person.

Sometimes when I've lost something, I'll ask the Holy Spirit where it is (because He knows everything, you know!). And I'll get a thought like, "Go look under the front seat of the car." Now, my mind might say, "That's silly. It couldn't be there." But when I look, there it is! The idea comes to me as a thought, but it's actually the inward witness, and it guides me where I need to go.

One time many years ago I was driving on a long trip by myself. I started to get sleepy, so I just pulled over to the side of the road, leaned my seat back, and took a little nap. I don't know how long I'd been sleeping when, suddenly, I woke with a start and felt like the Holy Spirit said to me, "Move—now." So I started the car and drove away.

And that's the end of the story! Who knows what might have happened if I hadn't moved. Maybe a tired trucker would have veered off the road right where I was parked and squished my little Honda like a bug. I don't know. But the Holy Spirit knows. He is inside us to lead us, guide us, and help us. Following the inward witness is vital.

Another time, I was on my way to a meeting, which was quite a few miles from my home. Suddenly, while I was driving along, I just had a "knowing in my knower" that I had left the stove on at my house. I can only describe it as an urgent thought that came out of the blue—and I recognized it as the prompting of the Holy Spirit.

Now, let me just say that I try to follow those promptings every single time. And there have been times when I've followed them and nothing happened—like I'll check and find that I *hadn't* left the stove on or forgotten anything. But I'd rather be safe than sorry, wouldn't you? Because there have also been times when I felt the prompting and I didn't do anything about it, only to look back afterward and say, "Oh, phooey, that *was* the Holy Spirit trying to help me!"

That happened recently when I was headed to the salon to have my hair cut. Just before I left home I felt the inward witness to take my laptop along. But I didn't do it. Then the whole time I was having my hair done I was thinking, "I want to go to the coffee place next door and write for a while—but I didn't bring my laptop!" As it turned out, when I was finished at the salon, I drove all the way back home to *get* my laptop, and then had a happy afternoon of writing at the coffee place. But it would have been so much easier and quicker if I had just obeyed the inward witness of the Holy Spirit!

As for the day when I got the urgent prompting about my stove—it was too far for me to go back to the house and still arrive on time to my meeting, so I called my neighbor and asked if she would check inside for me. In a few minutes she called back to let me know that, sure enough, I had left a saucepan of eggs boiling on the stove. By the time she got to it, the water had boiled dry, the eggs had exploded, and the pan was glowing red! She was able to turn off the stove before anything caught fire. And, bless her heart, she cleaned up the mess for me.

Thank God for the Holy Spirit's prompting! If I hadn't listened and called my neighbor, my house could have burned down. It really pays to practice listening to the inward witness. The Spirit rescues us when we've done something dumb. He is our Helper!

Those may be examples of small things, but it's good to practice on small things. When I'm making major decisions, I often will give myself more time to listen for the inward witness. I will let the Lord solidify the word in my spirit, and then I'll "try it on" before making a move one way or the other. We'll talk more about that in Key #4—Try It On.

Only One Thing Is Needed

Have you ever had so many things racing through your head that you couldn't make any decision at all, much less hear God's voice about it? I have! In my mind the conversation sort of sounds like this: "If I do it *this* way, then I won't be able to do *that* thing. But if I choose this *other* way, then it might lead to *this*—or I'll look like a fool. But if I don't do *this*, then there won't be enough resources to make sure *that* happens." (And on it goes.)

Know what I mean? It seems like fifty things need to happen

before the right decision can be made and you don't even know where to start.

I've learned that when I get to the point that too many thoughts are racing through my head for me to make a decision, then it's time to just *stop*. I know I've gotten too far off track and I'm trying to do too many things in my own strength. At that point I need to shut everything off and just get with the Lord to find out where I am and what needs to be done.

There's a story in Luke 10 that illustrates what I mean. At the end of the chapter Jesus has gone to visit Mary and Martha at their house in Bethany. Now, when Jesus comes to visit you, He doesn't come by Himself. There were at least twelve other guys with Him (the disciples) and probably quite a few more hangers-on, since He pretty much attracted a crowd wherever He went. So the task of fixing dinner for this entire gang fell on Mary and Martha. And I don't think Jesus called ahead for reservations! He came on a moment's notice.

What happened, though, is that Martha ended up in the kitchen doing most of the work because Mary decided to take full advantage of having the Lord at her house. She chose to sit at Jesus's feet and listen to Him (v. 39).

I can just imagine Martha in the kitchen, dashing about, peeling the potatoes, stirring the soup, making the salad, keeping an eye on the meat, trying to get everything to finish cooking at the same time—plus setting the table and coordinating the drinks. I feel for her! Then she realized that Mary wasn't even helping.

Now, we've all been there. We've all been in Martha's shoes—when there's too much to do and not enough time to do it and we realize that someone else on the team is not pulling their weight. It can be *really* irritating. Imagine the thoughts running through Martha's head. None of them were nice, I'm sure.

She was thinking about the fifty things she needed to do to get the dinner on the table—without Mary's help!

I can imagine the veins starting to stand out in her neck. And she worked herself into such a state of frustration that she dashed out to the living room and said point-blank to Jesus (probably in a rather strident voice): "Tell my sister to help me!" (See verse 40.) You know you're in the flesh when you run into your living room and yell at the Lord!

But Jesus told Martha something right then that always reminds me of what to do when *I* have too many things racing through my mind, especially at a time when I'm trying to make a decision. He said, "Martha, Martha [can't you just hear His placating yet compassionate tone?], you are worried and troubled about many things. But *one thing is needed*, and Mary has chosen that good part, which will not be taken away from her" (Luke 10:41–42, emphasis added).

Now, Martha thought a *lot* of things were needed. Everything needed to finish cooking, the salad needed to be made, the table needed to be set, the drinks needed to be poured—and Mary needed to get off her tushie and help!

But Jesus bypassed all that noise going on in Martha's head and said that only *one thing* was needed—and that Mary had chosen it.

What did she choose?

She chose to sit at His feet. To listen to Him. To seek Him. And what she received from that could never be taken away from her.

That always helps me. When my mind is racing and I think there are a hundred things that have to be done before I can reach a decision, Jesus says there's only one thing—to sit at His feet (seek Him and listen to Him). Then I can hear His voice and get His leading.

When I'm trying to do too many things in my own ability, or when I'm just overwhelmed by all the choices and voices, I know it's time to stop, spend time with Him, and listen to how He says to do it.

Set Your Day Straight

I can't tell you how many times this has worked for me. When God gives us His supernatural help with something, He makes things fall into place so much better than you or I ever could.

I remember one time when I had about a hundred things on my to-do list. I was stressed—so stressed, in fact, that I was planning to skip my morning devotions because I didn't have time for them. But I felt the Holy Spirit gently prompt me, "Karen, if you'll put Me first, I can set your day straight." So I went ahead and read my Bible and prayed before I headed out for the day.

> God makes things fall into place so
> much better than you or I ever could.

My first stop was the local superstore, where I had to pick up some oil for a hinge. Now, my apologies if you work at a store like that, but I have sort of a love-hate relationship with them. For one thing, they're just so huge. I have to walk for miles and miles looking for things, and that just eats up time. For another thing, there are sixteen checkout stands but *only two are ever open.* So the lines are long, and the checkers seem to move in slow motion.

I wasn't sure where the hinge oil might be in the store, and I was prepared for a long walk and then a long wait at the checkout line. But! I had that promise from the Holy Spirit: "If you'll put Me first, I can set your day straight."

And do you know what happened? I walked into the store and right there, on the endcap of the first aisle I came to, was the oil! I grabbed it and headed for the checkout stand where, lo and behold, no people were in line and the nice checker was standing out front motioning me toward her. I was in and out of that store in less than five minutes. Talk about a miracle! I had put God first, and He supernaturally helped set my day straight.

That might seem like a minor miracle to you, but it was thrilling to me. Imagine if God ordered every hour of every day like that for us! Just remember, whether your mind is racing from your to-do list or from trying to make just one decision, only one thing is needed: seeking God and getting His help. You might just get to see a miracle too. Think about this: In Luke 9, the chapter before Mary and Martha's story, Jesus had just fed a huge crowd of people using only five loaves and two fish (vv. 10–17). He knew all about how to feed a crowd in a miraculous way. I wonder if Martha, by taking on all the dinner prep in her own natural strength, missed her own crowd-feeding miracle. If she had chosen to sit at Jesus's feet and obtain the one needed thing (His wisdom and help), I wonder if Jesus would have provided dinner for everyone that day and they could have been witnesses to another miracle of multiplication.

I wonder if you and I have ever missed a miracle because we were trying to handle things in our own natural strength. I don't know about you, but that makes me want to stop more often and spend time in God's presence to hear His voice, rather than run amok while trying to get everything done on my own.

Where God Guides, He Provides

Sometimes, when we're facing a decision, the pressure is on us because the decision either has to be made within a time limit or it involves lots of money. When my first book, *Why, God, Why? What to Do When Life Doesn't Make Sense,* was coming out in 2013, I needed to decide whether or not to employ a public relations firm to help with the marketing before the book released. And, of course, I needed to decide *right then* because the work needed to start.

Now, hiring a PR firm to do a lot of the marketing work for you may sound like a great idea, but let me say this—it's not cheap. Every month (for at least six months, maybe more) it was going to cost *way* more than my paycheck could cover. I would have to believe God for the extra money—and we're not talking about just a few dollars.

My first thought was, "I can't afford it." But I've been practicing God's Word long enough to know that when I have that thought, it needs to be cast down! (See 2 Corinthians 10:5.) That is a limiting thought, and I don't ever want to put limits on God. He is the God who is more than enough. I knew He wasn't freaked out about the monthly bill I would have to undertake to hire the firm.

Now that doesn't mean you should just jump on every opportunity that costs a lot—just because God can cover it. No! I've seen too many people, and maybe you have too, who get into terrible financial trouble by taking on a huge overhead or buying something on credit, saying, "We'll just believe God for the money." That is foolishness if you haven't gotten God's specific go-ahead. As I mentioned before, where God guides, He provides—but first be sure He's guiding! God will provide for you *if* you're going in the direction He has told you to go.

And let me just say this: if you aren't a giver of tithes and offerings, don't try believing God for money. (See 2 Corinthians 9:6.) You must be involved in His economy, by sowing, if you want the principle of reaping to work for you.

So I sought God's direction about hiring the PR firm. I prayed, "Father, should I hire them to market my book? It's expensive, but I know You can supply all my need according to your riches in glory by Christ Jesus, as Philippians 4:19 says. Let me know what I should do."

Then every time I thought about it for the next couple days, I just said, "Thank You, Lord. You are showing me whether or not to hire this firm. I have Your guidance on it."

And here's what happened. Every day I read a scripture or had a conversation with someone or listened to a sermon that pointed to a yes answer from God. The Lord just kept sending things across my path that filled me with faith that I could do it. One sermon I listened to was about believing God for the impossible. (See Luke 1:37.) One friend I talked with told me an amazing story of God's provision. When I was reading the Bible, I came across the story about when Peter walked on water and I felt like the Lord said to me, "Karen, you can't walk on water if you don't get out of the boat."

Isn't that the truth? I knew He was telling me by the inward witness: "You won't get to see what happens if you don't take the first step. Come on, do you have faith or not? Get out of the boat!" And the faith rose up inside me.

It was scary, just as it probably was for Peter, but faith came from hearing God's Word. If I hadn't been reading my Bible, I wouldn't have seen that story right when I needed it, and God wouldn't have whispered His challenge to me. When we're seeking His direction, especially if a deadline is involved, we must put ourselves into position to hear His voice.

So I said yes to the PR firm and started paying that big

chunk of cash every month. And do you know what? Every month the bill got paid! Extra money kept coming in from unexpected sources month by month, and I had enough to pay the bill every time. In fact, I ended up continuing my contract with the PR firm for a couple more months, which cost even *more*, but the money was always there.

That's just one story of hearing God's voice to make the right decision. Pray and ask God for His direction. Keep saying and believing that you receive His direction. Then keep yourself in position by reading the Word and listening to other faith-filled people. It has worked in my life, and it will work in yours.

REVIEW IN A NUTSHELL

Jesus is our shepherd, and we really can hear and recognize His voice to lead us. When we get familiar with His Word by spending time with Him, we get better and better at following His promptings through the inward witness.

NOW ENGAGE:

Read and meditate on the scriptures we've looked at. Activate the power of God's Word in your life by speaking these declarations aloud:

> My sheep hear My voice, and I know them, and they follow Me.
> —JOHN 10:27

DECLARE: "Jesus is *my* good shepherd, and I can hear His voice! He knows me, and I recognize Him speaking to me, so I can follow Him. I follow the voice of God! I spend time in God's presence by reading His Word and praying so that He is free to speak to my heart and lead me."

⸙⸙⸙

> When he brings out his own sheep, he goes before them; and the sheep follow him, for they know his voice. Yet they will by no means follow a stranger, but will flee from him, for they do not know the voice of strangers.
> —JOHN 10:4–5

DECLARE: "I recognize and follow the voice of my shepherd, Jesus, and I won't follow the voice of any stranger, including the devil. I will get more and more familiar with His voice by spending time with Him—by reading His Word—because that is Him talking to me."

∽♋♋♋∾

For the word of God is living and powerful, and sharper than any two-edged sword, piercing even to the division of soul and spirit, and of joints and marrow, and is a discerner of the thoughts and intents of the heart.

—HEBREWS 4:12

DECLARE: "When I'm reading the Bible, I'm experiencing God's life and familiarizing myself with all that He is and all that He has for me. It's my covenant, and I'm getting more and more familiar with it so I know what belongs to me. When I'm well versed in the real thing, I can easily recognize a counterfeit."

∽♋♋♋∾

Martha, Martha, you are worried and troubled about many things. But one thing is needed, and Mary has chosen that good part, which will not be taken away from her.

—LUKE 10:41–42

DECLARE: "When I have too many things running through my head while trying to make a decision, I will remember to stop and sit at Jesus's feet instead of trying to fix everything in my own strength. I will remember that only *one* thing is needed in this situation: seeking Him. I won't get overwhelmed by all the details. I won't miss my miracle!"

WATCH YOUR MOUTH

Have you ever heard someone pray for something, then go right out and start saying exactly the opposite of what they prayed for? I have. For example, I've heard people ask God for direction in life, then heard them saying: "I can't hear from God. I have no idea what decision to make. It's so hard to know God's will."

We might call that "talking out of both sides of their mouth." In other words, they're undoing everything they prayed for by what they're saying! They believe more in what's happening (or not happening) around them than in the Word regarding God's direction, and they're undoing their prayer by what they're saying with their mouths.

I'm sure you've heard parents say to their child, "Watch your mouth." What do they mean by that? They mean, "Be careful what you're saying right now—it could get you into trouble!"

The same is true in spiritual things. When we're believing God for direction in our lives and asking Him to help us make right decisions, we want to be careful of what we're saying. We want *our* words to agree with *His* Word. In the decision-making process, it's important to speak words of faith, which simply means agreeing with the Bible. We agree with the Bible when we say what it says and nothing else. We water the seeds of faith by declaring God's Word in our lives.

Why Agree With the Bible

The Bible is our answer book. It's where we get a vision for our lives. If you want to find out what God thinks about something, go to His Word, the Bible. It's His guidebook on all the affairs of life. It shows us the way to go. Hebrews 4:12 says in the NIV that His word is "alive," and *The Message* adds that "His powerful Word is sharp as a surgeon's scalpel, cutting through everything." Another way to say it is, the Bible is what separates the truth from untruth. In other words, we need to watch what we're saying. We don't want to see the good news in the Bible, pray and ask God to bring it to pass in our lives, then go out and *say* exactly the opposite of what we just asked for.

> We agree with the Bible when we
> say what it says and nothing else.

That's easy to do if the situation looks bad or the circumstances say exactly the opposite of what we prayed for, but that's not what faith is. Faith is believing what God has said no matter what we see or feel. *That* is the fight of faith.

You see, there is creative power in your words. God Himself created the entire universe with words. Read Genesis 1:3 and you will see that "God said, 'Let there be light'; and there was light." He created light with words.

Amazingly God has given that same power to you. There is creative power in *your* words too. Mark 11:23 says it like this: "For assuredly, I say to you, whoever says to this mountain, 'Be removed and be cast into the sea,' and does not doubt in his heart, but believes that those things he says will be done, *he will have whatever he says*" (emphasis added).

That's amazing, isn't it? You will have whatever you've been saying! James 3 says it this way, comparing the tongue (our words) to the rudder of a ship: "Look also at ships: although they are so large and are driven by fierce winds, they are turned by a very small rudder wherever the pilot desires. Even so the tongue is a little member and boasts great things" (vv. 4–5). Your tiny tongue—or what you say—directs your life, just like a tiny rudder directs an entire ship.

So we all need to start watching our mouths!

Take a good, hard look at what you've been saying and make sure you're saying what God says. Agree with His Word by saying what it says instead of what you feel or see. Get *your* words in agreement with *His* Word. That's where the power of faith really begins to work for you.

Call for What You Want

Romans 4:17 says that God "calls those things which do not exist as though they did." In context, God is talking in this verse about Abram, the Old Testament patriarch who is the father of our faith. Abram didn't have any children, and he wanted a son more than anything (Gen. 15:2–3). God promised Abram and his wife, Sarai—when they were elderly—that they would have a multitude of children (Gen. 17:3–8).

It didn't happen, though, until God changed Abram's name to Abraham, which means "Father of nations." God started *calling* him a father before he *was* a father. Then it wasn't long until Abraham's son Isaac was born. God called him a father *by faith*, and then he became one.

That's what Romans 4:17 is talking about. God calls things that don't exist yet as though they do. And that's what He wants you to do as well. He wants you to call something that doesn't exist yet *as though it does.*

Mark 11:24 says, "Whatever things you ask when you pray, believe that you receive them, and you will have them." You do the believing when you pray—you believe what God has said *before* you see the answer to your prayer. For example, you believe that you're healed according to God's Word in 1 Peter 2:24 and Matthew 8:17 before you look or feel healed. And according to Romans 4:17, then you start *saying* what you believe before you *see* it. You call for what doesn't exist yet in the natural realm to come to pass in the natural (in this case, your healing).

When you've prayed for healing, you don't want to start saying, "Well, I prayed and I don't see it, so my prayer didn't work." When you've prayed and asked for God's direction for your life, you don't want to say, "He isn't answering me." Instead you want to get into agreement with God's Word. You want to say, "I believe I receive it now."

In other words, the Bible says to call for what you want, not what you have. Get into agreement with the Bible. If you want your dog Fido to come over to you, you don't say, "Here kitty, kitty, kitty." You also don't say, "Scat!" do you? No, you *say* what you want. You say, "Come here, Fido."

To make right decisions in your life, you need to stop saying, "I can't hear from God" and "I don't know what to do." Start saying you're led and you know which way to go, because that's what the Bible says in all the scriptures we've looked at. Say what you want, not what you have! Get your words into agreement with what you believe and with what the Bible says.

For example, we've seen how the Bible says that you hear the voice of God (John 10:27) and you know Him (John 14:17). Don't disagree with that by saying, "I don't know if I can hear

God's voice." The Bible says you do hear His voice! Start saying what it says.

The Bible says you are led by the Spirit of God (Rom. 8:14). Keep your words in line with God's Word. Say: "He is leading and guiding me right now. He's helping me make the right decision. I am led by His Spirit and I know what to do!" But don't say: "I'm not sure what direction to take." Clearly there is power in your words. Start using your tongue for good, not for evil!

One of my favorite examples of this involves the young man who owns the shop where I get my nails done. After I went to his shop for the first time and made an appointment, he handed me a business card. Along with the name of the shop and contact information, the card read, "Come happy. Leave happier." I thought that was a catchy slogan, but I soon learned it was much more.

> There is power in your words. Start
> using your tongue for good!

The first time he did my nails, he must have told me five times: "We make our clients happy," and "No one leaves here unhappy with their nails." As he worked, he looked me in the eye and said with a smile, "You will be happy with the job I do on your nails." He said it to the other nail techs and he said it to other clients who were having their nails done. On my next visit he said it, and at every other visit since then he has said it again and again.

That young man has figured out the power in his words! Since he opened his shop, he has been calling for what he wants, and guess what he now has? Happy clients! I know several women who go there, and they have no complaints. All of them are very happy with their nails.

I believe his words inspire him and his other techs to do a good job every day, and they inspire his clients to be happy. I've been to a lot of nail salons in my day, but I've never seen one so full of happy clients. We really can have what we say!

According to Proverbs 18:21, "Death and life are in the power of the tongue, and those who love it will eat its fruit"—meaning, you will "eat the fruit," or see the results, of what you've been saying. That verse is talking about *your* tongue. Speaking death (doubt) or speaking life (faith) is in the power of *your* tongue, not anyone else's. No one else is going to do this for you. It's up to you to speak words that agree with God's Word.

But that actually is good news—because it means you can choose! You are not a victim, and no one can stop this power from working in your life. You are the only one who speaks from your mouth. You can choose to speak words of death and doubt that agree with your circumstance, or you can speak words of life and faith that agree with the Bible.

Maybe you've asked God for help with the decisions you are facing. If so, what kind of words have you spoken about those decisions since then?

My Son's Story

When my youngest son, Ryan, was about to graduate from college, he had all sorts of decisions to make, just as most young people do after high school or college. He had been praying and asking God for direction for the next step in his life. But as the last term drew closer, he still didn't know what to do. He was in what I call "waiting mode."

Of course, well-meaning friends and relatives asked him all the time, just as we all ask a pending graduate: "What are you going to do after graduation?" And he just had to keep saying, "I don't know." It was bugging him. He didn't want to say he didn't know—after all, he was praying and believing that he *would* know. But while he was waiting to hear from God, he didn't want to keep speaking words that went against what he was believing for. He wanted what he was saying to agree with the Bible.

One day he finally hit on the answer. He was excited when he told me, "Mom, I know what to say now when people ask me what I'm going to do after graduation. I'll just answer them, 'I'll know when the time comes.'"

I thought that was a brilliant solution! It was a truthful answer that kept his words in line with what he had prayed and kept his faith on the answer. He didn't know what he was going to do, but he called for what he wanted, not what he had. And, lo and behold, by the time graduation came around, he had gotten a job offer from the university he attended. He knew it was the direction God wanted him to go, and he went to work for them as a recruiter for two years.

Waiting Mode

Now, let me just pause and say a word about waiting mode while we're here. I've heard a lot of people say, "I'm waiting on the Lord." They quote scriptures such as Isaiah 40:31, "Those who wait on the LORD shall renew their strength," or Psalm 27:14, "Wait on the LORD; be of good courage, and He shall strengthen your heart; wait, I say, on the LORD!" But let's be sure we understand what "waiting on the Lord" means.

First of all, waiting on the Lord *doesn't* mean sitting on the couch watching TV and eating candy while you wait for God to show up and speak to you in an audible voice. And it doesn't mean just going about your business, passively wondering if or when God will send the answer. Far from it!

> We need to know what to do
> between "Amen" and "There it is!"

Yes, many times there is a waiting period between your prayer and your answer. We all like it when we see results immediately, but maybe you've noticed, as I have, that most of the time things don't happen as fast as we want them to. We are the children of a "have it now" society. We have microwaves and drive-through windows and instant information in the palm of our hands via search engines. We want everything *now!*

But sometimes we must wait. And we need to know how to stay in faith during waiting mode. I like the way one minister puts it: we need to know what to do between "Amen" and "There it is!"

Waiting on the Lord is *not* relaxing or even passively accepting the circumstances. Instead, it is very active. The Merriam-Webster dictionary offers several definitions of the word *wait*, including "to stay in place in expectation of" and "to remain stationary in readiness." It also says "to look forward expectantly" and "to be ready and available." That's not somebody just sitting around, is it?

No, waiting on the Lord means you're expectantly looking forward to your answer. The best way to do that is to actively speak words of faith that agree with the Bible. Continually say that God is working on your situation. Don't say something that's opposite of what you've prayed for. Be hopeful, believing the answer is just around the corner, due to arrive any minute.

This waiting isn't lazy and doesn't put everything on hold. I like something the famous painter Leonardo da Vinci once said: "Iron rusts from disuse, stagnant water loses its purity and in cold weather becomes frozen; even so does inaction sap the vigor of the mind." Don't sit around waiting for God to do something. Let Him find you busy!

So, the kind of waiting the Bible is talking about is an *active* waiting. It has you waking up every morning expecting to find the answer. It's like when a woman is pregnant. We say she is "expecting" a baby. Everyone can see that the promise of a baby is inside her. Now, we can't see the baby itself yet, but we know it's there.

And what does this "expectant" mother spend her days doing while she's waiting? She plans for her baby's arrival. She collects baby clothes and diapers and starts getting the nursery ready. Why? She's expecting a baby to arrive! She knows the promise will be fulfilled—it's just a matter of time. She is expectant and she'll wait as long as it takes.

This word *wait* also has another active connotation. *Strong's Exhaustive Concordance* renders one definition as "wait (for, on, upon)." It is the Hebrew word *qâvâh*, which is used in Psalm 27:14: "Wait on the LORD; be of good courage, and He shall strengthen your heart; wait, I say, on the LORD!"

Think of *waiting* like being a server who waits on tables at a restaurant. There's nothing relaxing about being a waiter or waitress! If you've ever been one, you know it's hard work that requires all your attention and energy. There is a lot of serving going on.

So the act of waiting on the Lord isn't spent sitting around, passively hoping that something will happen sometime soon. You must be eagerly awaiting God's answer. You're actively serving, trusting, and speaking words that agree with His

Word. Waiting mode is a crucial time of faith. Your words are more important than ever while you're between "Amen" and "There it is!"

Hung by the Tongue

In his book *Hung by the Tongue* Francis P. Martin says, "What you say is what you get." What a powerful truth! It makes me want to ask myself what I've been getting, because then I have to ask myself what I've been saying.

The great thing about that is, I get to decide. I am the only one in control of what I say, and so are you. We can either be hung by our tongue or use it to speak words of life and agreement with God. Which are you doing on a consistent basis?

There is a well-known saying that has been attributed to several different people, and it goes something like this: "He who says he can and he who says he can't are both usually right." It's true, isn't it? Your words have great power! What are you saying? If you say you can, then your faith is working. You're agreeing with God and with His Word. As Christians, we must learn to use our words effectively—we must agree with what God says and not speak words that are contrary to the Bible, especially if we're in waiting mode.

We've all done it from time to time—we've all been taken captive by our words. We've said things like, "It's not working," or "Where is God in all this?", or "Why doesn't He answer me?" And then we bear the fruit of discouragement, doubt, and confusion. Instead of getting God's direction for our lives and His help with decisions, we end up wandering and wondering.

I encourage you to check up on what you've been saying. If you recognize that you've been in *disagreement* with God's Word, don't feel bad or guilty. Just decide right now to change! Start speaking words of faith. Do as my son Ryan did and change what you're saying. Start saying things such as, "I believe God is directing me," and "Even now He's working all things together for my good, as Romans 8:28 says." You can decide today to watch your mouth and let your words agree with the Bible!

REVIEW IN A NUTSHELL

It's important that we watch our mouths and keep our words in agreement with God's Word, because we don't want to undo everything we've prayed for. There is power in our words!

NOW ENGAGE

Read and meditate on the scriptures we've looked at. Activate the power of God's Word in your life by speaking these declarations aloud:

> Sanctify them by Your truth. Your word is truth.
>
> —JOHN 17:17

DECLARE: "Since the Bible is absolute truth, it will set me free in every area of my life. God loves me and knows just how to guide me, so I will watch my mouth and stay in agreement with His Word. I'll say what He says. I won't speak words that disagree with the Bible."

⌦⌦⌦

> For assuredly, I say to you, whoever says to this mountain, "Be removed and be cast into the sea," and does not doubt in his heart, but believes that those things he says will be done, he will have whatever he says.
>
> —MARK 11:23

DECLARE: "There is creative power in the words I speak, so I am going to watch what I say. I speak words that agree with what I've prayed and asked for. I can have whatever I say, so I say that God is directing me and helping me make the right decisions!"

God...calls those things which do not exist as though
they did.
                                                 —ROMANS 4:17

DECLARE: "Right now the right decision might not be evi-
dent, but I'm going to do what God did and call for what I
want. Father, thank You that Your plan is coming to pass in
my life. I hear Your voice and follow Your leading. This is all
turning out for my good!"

Death and life are in the power of the tongue, and those
who love it will eat its fruit.
                                                 —PROVERBS 18:21

DECLARE: "Because my words have power I'm going to speak
words of life and I will see the results of what I say. No one else
is going to do this for me, so I determine to speak words that
agree with God's Word. I'm not a victim, and no one can stop
this power from working in my life!"

Those who wait on the LORD shall renew their strength.
                                                 —ISAIAH 40:31

DECLARE: "When I am in waiting mode I will continue to
look forward expectantly to receiving God's direction. I know
that God is working on my situation. I will serve and trust and
continue to speak words of faith that agree with His Word. I
won't talk out of both sides of my mouth or speak words of
doubt. This is a crucial time of faith when my words are more
important than ever between 'Amen' and 'There it is!'"

TRY IT ON

W HEN YOU GO to the store to buy a new shirt, you usually try it on first, right? That's how you know if it fits you well or if it looks as good on you as it did on the mannequin. I've bought a few shirts in my day that I *didn't* try on first, only to get home and find out they just weren't right for me. Then I had to take them back. It always pays to try things on before you commit to them.

The same is true when it comes to making a decision. It only makes sense to "try it on" first before you commit to it. By that I mean you should do something for the Holy Spirit to witness to, or "confirm," for you. Take some steps in a direction and see how it sits with your spirit and the Holy Spirit.

It always pays to try things on
before you commit to them.

This is the same way you know you're saved. Romans 8:16 says, "The Spirit Himself bears witness with our spirit that we are children of God." The Holy Spirit can also bear witness

81

with your spirit when it comes to making the right decisions for your life.

Take Some Steps

Let's say you're trying to decide whether or not to move to a new city. Instead of just sitting on your couch reading your Bible, or kneeling in your prayer closet, start to take some steps in the direction of the new city. Now don't misunderstand me, reading the Bible on your couch and kneeling in your prayer closet are vitally important to your decision-making process.

But it's important in addition to get up and *do* something, to see if the Lord really is leading you in a certain direction. Try it on—take some steps and give the Holy Spirit something to say yes or no to! Luke, the author of the Book of Acts, says more than once that the disciples moved ahead with a plan because it seemed good to them *and* to the Holy Spirit (Acts 15:25, 28). Thank God for the Holy Spirit witnessing to us when we need His direction and help in deciding things.

> Keep taking steps until you either get a
> red light in your spirit or you're there!

For starters, you might go online and look at real estate in the new city—then check your spirit. By "check your spirit," I mean stop and put your spiritual antenna up. Ask God, "Does this seem right? Am I going in the right direction?" See how your spirit feels. Are you getting that smooth, velvety feeling or a scratchy feeling deep inside? That's your spirit giving witness to what you're trying on.

If you don't get a red light on the inside—the feeling that something's not quite right—then take another step. Maybe check out the schools in the new city or find out what church you would go to. (Always put your spiritual health first place in your decision!) Then stop and check your spirit again. Do you still have a green light? Then take another step.

Maybe your next step is to "spy out the land." By that I mean actually take a trip to visit the new city and check it out, just as the children of Israel did when they arrived at the Jordan River to cross into the Promised Land. Joshua sent a contingency into the land of Canaan to see what was there and charged them:

> See what the land is like: whether the people who dwell in it are strong or weak, few or many; whether the land they dwell in is good or bad; whether the cities they inhabit are like camps or strongholds; whether the land is rich or poor; and whether there are forests there or not. Be of good courage. And bring some of the fruit of the land.
>
> —NUMBERS 13:18–20

I always encourage people who are thinking about moving or taking a position at a ministry to first go there and spy out the land. Spend some time just *being* there, hanging out in the environment you're thinking of moving to. There's just no way you can know what's going on in a place if you don't visit. Even then you probably won't see everything that's happening, but when you're *in* a place, you can get a good sense of whether or not you fit there. When you visit the new place, stop frequently and check with the Holy Spirit. Ask Him, "Is this right? Should I keep moving forward?"

The idea here is to just keep taking steps until you either get a red light in your spirit or you're there! When it comes to making major decisions like this, I will often take longer to listen. I'll try on many things, moving ahead step by step and keeping my spiritual antenna up, listening for God's voice. I will let Him solidify it in my spirit before making a move one way or the other.

If you want a new car, take a step and test-drive a few. If you think God is leading you to start a new business, get online and check out similar businesses, or get information from the US Small Business Administration. Maybe you're trying to decide whether or not to go back to school. To try that on, you might start with examining schools that have the programs you're interested in. Each time you check out a different one, stop to ask the Holy Spirit, "Is this one right?" If you don't get a no, then keep taking steps.

Many times when I am trying on a decision I will say something like, "OK, I'm going to do this"; then I'll stop to see how that settles in my spirit. I'll let a day or so go by, then I'll say, "OK, I'm *not* going to do this," and I'll see what the Holy Spirit tells my spirit. Am I getting that smooth, velvety feeling or a scratchy feeling? If I don't know, I keep checking until I know for sure whether or not to do it.

Follow After Peace

It's so important to be in a place of peace when you're making decisions. When you spend time reading and meditating on God's Word, it fills your life with peace. And that is the position from which you want to make decisions. Make every decision from a place of peace, not agitation. As you're "trying it on," make sure your heart is at peace before you take the next step.

One friend of mine says it like this: "When we live from a position of peace, we are not driven, beaten, or whipped by circumstances. We can think straight; we can take time to consider things and make good decisions. Peace of mind and peace of heart are priceless."

Colossians 3:15 says, "And let the peace of God rule in your hearts, to which also you were called in one body; and be thankful." The Good News Translation renders it this way: "The peace that Christ gives is to guide you in the decisions you make." Isn't that good? Peace helps to guide you in your decisions.

The Amplified Bible gives us further insight into that verse: "And let the peace (soul harmony which comes) from Christ rule (act as umpire continually) in your hearts [deciding and settling with finality all questions that arise in your minds]."

Peace helps to guide you
in your decisions.

I love that image of peace acting as the umpire of our lives. In a baseball game, what does an umpire do? He's the guy who runs the game and makes all the calls. If the umpire says you're out, then you're out, no matter what you or anyone else thinks about it. The umpire's word is law—his choices and decisions always stand. There's no doubt in anyone's mind about who is in charge of the game.

I've seen team managers charge onto the field and shout right in an umpire's face when they disagree with a call. I've even seen them chest-bump each other! It's pretty hilarious to watch, but it's completely futile. The manager is not going to win because the umpire is in charge. He rules the game and always has the final say.

Have you ever watched a manager get into a shouting match with an ump and then seen the umpire back off and say, "OK, coach, you're right. I'll change the call"? Of course not! Because you can yell at an umpire all you want, but he's always going to win the argument. Very often, in fact, the umpire throws the manager out of the game for his behavior.

This verse in the Amplified Bible is telling us to let *peace* be the umpire of our lives. Let peace be in charge. Let *it* rule, let *it* have the final say. Follow after peace. To me, doing that is a threefold concept.

First, it means that decisions should be made from a position of peace, not agitation. Get your heart and mind quiet, perhaps by reading the Word or praying in the spirit, so you can clearly hear from God.

Second, following after peace means that when you try on a decision you feel the peace of God in your spirit (that smooth, velvety feeling) and you go with it.

<hr>

Get your heart and mind quiet so
you can clearly hear from God.

<hr>

Third, peace keeps you in a place of faith as you watch your decision unfold. It keeps you from second-guessing yourself or changing your mind every other minute. Peace keeps you on track. It keeps you from fretting about decisions you've made. Philippians 4:6–7 tells us:

> Be anxious for nothing, but in everything by prayer
> and supplication, with thanksgiving, let your requests
> be made known to God; and the peace of God, which
> surpasses all understanding, will guard your hearts and
> minds through Christ Jesus.

God's peace comes when you pray and refuse to be anxious. That peace will guard your heart and mind so you can keep it throughout the decision-making process and after you've made your decision.

Launch Out

The main idea of "trying it on" is to do something, to give the Holy Spirit something to witness to. It's the same theory that says you can't steer a parked car. It's much easier for the Holy Spirit to steer us when we're already moving in a direction. I envision it like this: you have to be moving in a certain direction in the *natural* for God to come along and add His *super* to it. Then you have the *supernatural*!

For example, a ship at anchor never catches the wind—only the ships that have launched out and are headed in a direction will catch the wind when it comes up. They're the only ones that will actually make the trip and end up where they're supposed to be. The ship that stays anchored in the harbor never gets anywhere.

Your part and mine is to take a step. Try it on. Launch out. Then check with the Holy Spirit to see if you are taking the right direction. If you stay in one place—if you keep your anchor down—you may never take any steps of faith and never end up at your divine destination.

Sometimes it's scary to get moving. There is risk involved. But I once heard someone say that while ships in the harbor may be safe, ships weren't built to sit in the harbor. No, they are meant to sail on the open waters—just as you are meant to "sail" a course with God! You weren't handcrafted and gifted by God to do nothing. Don't be afraid to launch out.

That's what Jesus told Peter to do in Luke 5. He knew Peter had fished all night and caught absolutely nothing, so He borrowed Peter's boat that bright, early morning, pushed off a little from the shore, and taught the Word to a crowd of people. When He was finished preaching, He said to Peter, "Launch out into the deep and let down your nets for a catch" (Luke 5:4).

Now, Peter didn't want to do it. He was discouraged from a long night of unfruitful work. He was probably tired and hungry and wanted nothing more than to go home to bed. He said, "Master, we have toiled all night and caught nothing" (v. 5). Peter knew that morning fishing was a ridiculous idea. In the Sea of Galilee fish can see the shadow of the boat on the water when the sun is up, so no fisherman in his right mind would fish in the morning. That's why he'd gone out at night.

But Jesus knew something Peter didn't. He knew the only way to rectify a night of fruitless fishing was to launch out—because that's where the miracle catch was waiting. He was trying to get a blessing to Peter, but it was going to require some effort on Peter's part. And it was going to require faith, because in the natural there was no way to catch fish in the morning.

Realize that the fulfilling of your divine destiny will take some effort on your part.

To Peter's credit, he didn't turn the Lord down. He took the step of faith and said, "Nevertheless at Your word I will let down the net" (v. 5). He rallied his weary crew and launched out into the deep. And you know what happened. The Bible says:

When they had done this, they caught a great number of fish, and their net was breaking. So they signaled to their partners in the other boat to come and help them. And

they came and filled both the boats, so that they began
to sink.

—LUKE 5:6–7

Because Peter was willing to put action to his faith and do
his part by launching out, he received a net-breaking, boat-
sinking miracle! The same can happen to you when you're
willing to step out, get moving in a direction, and try on the
direction you're feeling in your spirit.

So be brave and launch out! Realize that the fulfilling of your
divine destiny will take some effort on your part. It's going to
require faith. Take some steps and ask God whether they're
right or not. He has great plans for you, so step out and meet
that plan.

REVIEW IN A NUTSHELL

When we're facing a major decision, it makes sense to try it on before committing to it. This gives the Holy Spirit an opportunity to witness to our spirit about whether or not we're going in the right direction. It will require effort on our part—but we can't be afraid to launch out.

NOW ENGAGE

Read and meditate on the scriptures we've looked at. Activate the power of God's Word in your life by speaking these declarations aloud:

> The Spirit Himself bears witness with our spirit that we
> are children of God.
> —ROMANS 8:16

DECLARE: "The Holy Spirit can bear witness with my spirit when it comes to making right decisions for my life. So I will 'try on' a decision first, before I commit to it."

◇◇◇

> For it seemed good to the Holy Spirit, and to us.
> —ACTS 15:28

DECLARE: "The Holy Spirit can witness to my spirit when I need His direction and help in deciding things. So I will do something for the Holy Spirit to witness to. I will take steps in a direction to see how that course sits with my spirit and with the Holy Spirit in me. I trust Him to lead and guide me."

❦

Send men to spy out the land of Canaan.... See what the
land is like.

—NUMBERS 13:2, 18

DECLARE: "When I'm trying to decide about a major move,
I will spy out the land. I'll spend some time just being there,
hanging out in the environment to see if I fit in with it. I will
frequently check with the Holy Spirit, asking Him if this is the
right place for me. Then I'll keep taking steps until I either get
a red light in my spirit or I'm there (knowing the Spirit has
given me the green light to be there)."

❦

And let the peace (soul harmony which comes) from
Christ rule (act as umpire continually) in your hearts
[deciding and settling with finality all questions that
arise in your minds].

—COLOSSIANS 3:15, AMP

DECLARE: "I will let peace be the umpire of my life. When I'm
making a decision, I'll make it from a position of peace, not agitation. I'll get my heart and mind quiet so I can clearly hear from
God. When I try a decision on, I'll look for the peace of God
in my spirit (that smooth, velvety feeling) and go with it. I'll let
peace keep me in a place of faith as I watch my decision unfold."

Launch out into the deep and let down your nets for a catch.
—LUKE 5:4

DECLARE: "I realize it's going to take some effort on my part to hear God's voice, make the right decision, and fulfill my divine destiny. I'm going to have to take some steps and start moving in a direction. I'm not afraid to launch out into the deep, because that's where my destiny is waiting!"

GET GOOD ADVICE

WHAT I'M ABOUT to say may or may not come as a revelation to you: you don't know everything. And thankfully there are *people* around you who have been through some things and might have some wisdom that will be helpful to you for making your decision. The Bible says we should seek some of these people out when we're making plans and decisions. "Without counsel, plans go awry, but in the multitude of counselors they are established" (Prov. 15:22).

Several brains are simply better than one. We need one another. Of course, when someone gives you advice, you should weigh it—while still relying on the Holy Spirit to lead and guide you. But none of us ever were meant to live the Christian life alone. There are times when we need to seek advice and, as the Bible says, imitate others as they imitate Christ. (See 1 Corinthians 11:1.)

Who to Ask

I fully believe that God places godly Christian mentors and advisers in your life, people for you to be accountable to. These are flesh-and-blood human beings who have godly wisdom and no other agenda than to help you. Some might be peers—good

Christian friends who know your weaknesses and will get in your face to ask you how it's going. Everyone needs a couple of good friends like that. If you don't have them now, ask God to send you one or two.

Some advisers might be older in the faith than you, spiritual overseers who have more experience and insight than you have. Some might be personal friends, while others might be pastors and teachers, set in the body of Christ by God to edify and perfect you (Eph. 4:11–12). Their advice might come from a pulpit or a podcast rather than face-to-face, but it is no less valuable.

Don't run from these advisers or ignore their advice. Thank God for them and listen when they instruct you.

Now, when it comes to getting direction and advice from "a multitude of counselors," the Bible is not talking about polling everyone you know. It's talking about asking counsel of those select few types of individuals we talked about—the people who will give you informed, insightful, and helpful advice with no strings attached. They should be those who love you and want the best for you.

If you start asking a lot of people for advice, you're going to get too many opinions, and that can get very confusing. As the old saying goes, "Too many cooks can spoil the broth." For example, I know some Christians who, when faced with crises or other prayer needs in their lives, will phone twenty or more prayer lines. I guess their rationale is that if one prayer is good, twenty are better!

But Matthew 18:19 says that "if two of you agree on earth concerning anything that they ask, it will be done for them by My Father in heaven." Notice that verse says it takes only two! In fact, the more people you get involved, the less chance there is of them all being in agreement. Think about this: if you ask twenty people to agree with you in prayer, what are the chances that *all* of them will stay in faith and agreement with you? Very little. Then the prayer of agreement won't work—because it says things get done by our Father when we *agree*.

I'd much rather find just one or two godly friends with faith and agree with them in prayer. It's the same when you get too many opinions about making a decision. Too many opinions muddy the waters. When it comes to asking for advice, it's better to aim for quality rather than quantity. Seek out those godly people God has placed in your life to help you, mentor you, and oversee your spiritual life.

We can see an example of this type of mentoring relationship in the New Testament between the apostle Paul and the young pastor Timothy. Throughout their relationship Paul challenges Timothy, equips him for ministerial tasks, empowers him for success, and chooses him as his successor. He admonishes Timothy to "flee the evil desires of youth," encourages him when people look down on him for being young, and bolsters Timothy's confidence when he is timid (2 Tim. 2:22; 1 Tim. 4:12; 2 Tim. 1:17).

> When it comes to asking for advice, it's better to aim for quality rather than quantity.

The evidence that you have a God-given mentor relationship with someone, as Timothy had with Paul, will be that your mentor will have a good track record in their own walk with the Lord—you'll see good fruit in their life and ministry. (See Matthew 12:33.) In addition, in their interaction with you they will be encouraging but honest and comforting but challenging, and their main goal will be your growth and success. When you have that kind of relationship with someone, you can, and should, ask for their advice—and you should follow it.

One Family's Story

I have some missionary friends who had lived and ministered in a certain country for more than twelve years when trouble developed there and the army of a neighboring nation invaded. It was a precarious time. My friends sought the Lord and asked advice from their leaders and other missionaries about whether they should stay or leave.

The situation became fairly dangerous, and they felt led to return to America for a while, a little bit ahead of their regular furlough schedule. So they left people in charge of their church and Bible school, gathered up their children and other American workers, and came home. They spent the summer itinerating and vacationing, much as they would have done under normal circumstances. They prayed for their mission country, and so did many of their church members and friends.

As the summer progressed and the time to head back to the mission field drew nearer, they sought the Lord big-time about whether to go back. Thankfully many changes had occurred in the nation due to prayer. Even in the natural, conditions were starting to get better. It looked as if they might be able to return without a problem.

I was so impressed, though, by the way they handled this major decision. They didn't just say, "We're people of faith! We're going back!" No, they sought the Lord's guidance, *and* they sought out the advice of several other missionaries and leaders in their ministerial organization. In midsummer they told me they had planned a meeting with the ministerial leader of their region, as well as the person from the home office who was above that leader. My friends said, "We aren't going to buy tickets or make any plans to return until we get the green light from them."

Keep in mind that they had been missionaries for many years. They themselves had given advice to many, many other missionaries. They also had put in a lot of prayer over this situation. They were well able to hear from God themselves—they'd done it many times before. In fact, you could say that on the mission field they lived by the leading of the Lord every day! For them, seeking God's guidance was a way of life and many times a matter of success or failure, even life or death. They had had lots of practice at hearing the voice of God and obeying Him.

In the natural there is safety in numbers,
but that is a supernatural fact as well.

But they also knew that in the midst of the situation they faced, all sorts of dynamics were going on, and what was really needed was the impartial, wise advice of others—those who were on the outside of the situation and weren't as invested in it. These wise missionaries knew that their emotions, their livelihood, their safety, their love for the people in that country all could have been tugging on them, causing them to make the wrong decision. So they humbly asked for advice from their leaders. There is so much wisdom in that.

We know that in the natural there is safety in numbers, but that is a supernatural fact as well. Proverbs 11:14 says it plainly: "In the multitude of counselors there is safety." It's a blessing to be in the *body* of Christ where we can get wise counsel from others and not have to make every major decision on our own.

If You're Giving the Advice

Let me just take a minute here to talk about *giving* godly advice. If someone sees you as their mentor, friend, or spiritual overseer and comes to you asking for your counsel, there are some important things you should know.

First of all, just by the act of asking for your advice, chances are pretty good that this person looks up to you and reveres you. You probably have a great deal of influence with them, so treat it respectfully. Realize they might be ready to act upon *any* advice you give them because of their relationship with you. So don't take it lightly and just blurt out something without seriously considering your answer first.

Merriam-Webster's dictionary defines *advice* as "an opinion or suggestion about what someone should do." Place an emphasis on *opinion* or *suggestion*. A person comes to you because of your experience, wisdom, or relationship with them—and hopefully because they know you care about them.

But you are not deciding for them. Remember, you are responsible to them, but you are not responsible for them. You want to guide and instruct them, not make their decisions for them.

I've heard about instances of extreme discipleship in the body of Christ in which younger Christians have been instructed to submit themselves to an elder or mentor for *every* decision they make. They aren't allowed to make any decision on their own, from where to attend school or what car to buy to how many children to have or whom to marry. That's not at all scriptural. As elders and advisers, our *main* goal should be helping other Christians align their lives with the Word of God and discern the leading of the Lord for themselves.

I rarely butt into someone's life with advice; rather, I wait for them to come to me. Now, that's not to say I haven't ever initiated advice, but usually only after a *very* strong unction from the Holy Spirit—like, He won't let me sleep until I seek this person out. Even then I don't come at them with all guns blazing, making it sound like I know everything they should or shouldn't be doing. I still tread softly to see if they're open to receiving counsel from me. Because if they're not, it doesn't matter how good my advice is, it will fall on deaf ears.

Remember, you are responsible to them,
but you are not responsible for them.

Many times we are called upon to give someone advice or counsel on a moment's notice. We have no way of knowing in advance what's going on with them. In other words, we haven't prayed about their situation, so we're giving advice completely from the natural standpoint. When that's the case, let the person know that the advice you're giving them is your *opinion*, not a prophetic "thus saith the Lord" unction. Of course, the Lord may have spoken to you, but if He hasn't, don't pin it on Him.

Very often when I'm giving someone counsel I'll also say something like, "If it were me, I might..." That way, by making it conditional, they still have a chance to weigh what I've said and see if it witnesses with them. That's what I want them to do anyway—I want them to seek God, learn how to hear His voice, and be led by the Holy Spirit for themselves.

In counseling, I've also said, "Here are some things you might want to consider..."

Talk to them about their options, good or bad. If someone is presenting an idea to you and it sounds good to you, it's OK to say, "That seems good to me, but the ultimate decision is yours."

Here's another important point: always lead them to the Word of God.

The Bible is their answer book, and if you can't back up your opinion or suggestion with the Word, then maybe it's not worth giving. Help them to see what the Word of God says about their situation. That way they'll know where to go for answers the next time they need counsel too.

Just remember, you aren't God. Guiding the course of someone's life is much too big a job for you or me. It's not up to you or me to tell a person what to do or to *make* him or her choose a particular course of action. That's the Holy Spirit's job. He's good at it—He's been doing it a long time, and we should trust Him to do it.

How to Ask

Now, back to asking someone for godly counsel. Proverbs 24:6 says, "By wise counsel you will wage your *own* war" (emphasis added).

The point is, this verse says you *do* have to wage your own war—no one else is going to do it for you. The purpose of an accountability partner or a counselor is not for them to tell you what to do. You *will* have to make your own decisions, with God's help. No matter how badly you might want someone to decide for you, that's not their responsibility. It's yours. But there is safety in getting the wisdom of others before you go off to fight the good fight of faith.

However, there is a way to ask for that counsel and a way not to. I'll show you what I mean.

When I first took over pastoring alone at our church in Boise, Idaho, God provided me with a wonderful pastor-mentor and his wife. They were dear friends. They helped me through the process. They had been pastors for a number of years, and they helped my staff and me in more ways than I can tell you. What a blessing they were! Anytime I needed pastoral advice they were on hand to help.

Guiding the course of someone's life
is much too big a job for you or me.

But one time I went to that pastor and said, "God told me to do such-and-such, so I'm going to do it." I can't even remember now what it was. At the time he just nodded and said, "OK." But when I did it, it turned out badly. Later when I was telling him about it, he said, "Yeah, I figured that would happen." Sort of miffed, I asked him, "Why in the world didn't you tell me that beforehand! Why did you just let me go ahead and do it?"

I'll never forget his answer. He said, "Because you didn't ask me, Karen. You came and said, 'God told me, so I'm going to do it.' What could I say to that?"

Wow. I learned a valuable lesson: when asking someone for advice, don't lead with "God told me..." That leaves your adviser no room to give their opinion or help you in any way.

Instead, I should have approached him by saying something like: "I feel like God might be leading me to do this. *What do you think*?" After all, that's why I was bringing the whole idea to him anyway, right? I wanted to know what he thought about it! I wanted to involve his insight and experience to help me determine whether or not what I thought was really a God-idea or not.

Don't do what I did! Give your adviser an opportunity to

give input. Approach them with humility and a desire to hear what they have to say.

Learn to Listen

Sometimes we ask for advice, but if we don't like the advice, we don't take it. It's so important when we get wise counsel that we follow it. Don't just seek out good advice, but also listen to it and act on it. I've been in more than one situation in which I've given someone advice they didn't like, and because of it they did just the opposite. Sadly things didn't turn out very well for them.

I've also had people make an appointment with me because they wanted to talk over some plans they had and get my input. But when they came, all they did was talk! They *told* me everything they wanted to do, never letting me get a word in edgewise. They never asked for my input at all.

Then, afterward, they went out and told everyone that (presumably because I was there when they were talking) I knew all about what they were doing and totally approved of it. That's so aggravating! They never once *asked* me; they just *told* me. Then they assumed that since I didn't jump in and correct them I approved of everything they were doing.

The thing about being accountable to someone is really very simple: you have to be accountable to them. You need to listen to them. Too many times I've seen Christians run away from the advisers God placed in their lives simply because the adviser gave advice they didn't want to follow. When their spiritual leader or their accountability partner said no, they didn't want to hear it; so they ignored it.

When I was younger (both in age and my faith walk) my spiritual father used to say, "Listen to what I'm telling you so you don't have to make the same mistakes I did. Just take my word for it!" I'm happy to say that sometimes I took that sage advice—but, sadly, sometimes I didn't.

~~~~~~~~~~~~~~~~~~~~~~~~~~~~~~~~~~~~~~
The thing about being accountable to
someone is, you have to be accountable.
~~~~~~~~~~~~~~~~~~~~~~~~~~~~~~~~~~~~~~

There's just something about us humans—sometimes we have to try things for ourselves and learn our life lessons the hard way, don't we? When we were young and someone said, "Whatever you do, don't touch that hot stove," what did we do? Nine times out of ten we just *had* to touch it, didn't we? And when we did, we found out they were right—it was hot and it burned us! But we had to find out the hard way.

I remember one time when I was just a little tyke, maybe five or six years old, I learned a lesson the hard way. My dad owned a hardware store, and he used to keep razor blades in his desk drawer, the kind you use in a box cutter. One day when I was fooling around in his desk drawer, I picked up the carton of razors and carefully looked them over. They were individually wrapped. I guess that made them seem like chewing gum or something, because they just looked so interesting to me.

My dad saw me looking at them and said, "Don't ever take those out of the cardboard and touch one, OK? They're really sharp."

"OK," I answered.

But from that moment on they fascinated me. I walked away from the desk but just kept thinking about those blades. I'd never seen razor blades in a cardboard sleeve before, and I really wanted to unwrap one. I just *had* to know how sharp they really were!

So when no one was looking, I went back to my dad's desk,

slowly opened the drawer, and gingerly took out one of the cardboard sleeves. With my heart racing, I turned it over and over in my hands, then carefully took the blade out of the sleeve and—you guessed it—I ran it right across my finger to see what would happen. To my horror, the skin split wide open, blood started pouring out, and it hurt like the dickens!

Of course, my dad picked that exact moment to come back into the office. He saw what had happened and grabbed my finger to stop the bleeding. Thankfully I didn't need stitches, but as he was patiently washing and bandaging the cut, he asked in disbelief, "Why did you do exactly what I told you not to do?"

Why, indeed? What is it about us humans that we don't want to take advice—especially good advice that will help prevent us from doing stupid things?

Submit Yourself

It takes some maturity to ask for someone's advice and then submit to their counsel. Sometimes our own pride will rise up and we'll think, "I don't have to listen to them. I hear from God too!" That's the same mentality Aaron and Miriam had in Numbers 12:2 when they rose up against Moses and said, "Has the LORD indeed spoken only through Moses? Has He not spoken through us also?"

Read further in the chapter and you'll see God heard them say it. Because He did, their little burst of pride didn't turn out very well. After God called them out to the tabernacle and read them the riot act, Miriam suddenly found she was covered with leprosy!

Now, I'm not saying that being too proud to seek advice will cause you to become a leper, but my point is this: yes, God does speak to you and through you, but there are times when all of us need to listen and submit ourselves to others. There are times when good advice comes from those around you, and it will pay you rich dividends to heed it, even if you don't like the advice initially. Don't be too proud to receive good counsel.

It takes some maturity to ask
for someone's advice and then
submit to their counsel.

I've even heard some Christians use verses in 1 John 2 as a reason they don't need to take advice from anyone. They'll say, "I have an unction from the Holy One, and I know all things. I don't need anyone to teach me—I'm anointed!" (See verses 20, 27.) That, as one minister used to say, is just ignorance gone to seed. Even worse, it's pride, and Proverbs 16:18 says, "Pride goes before destruction, and a haughty spirit before a fall."

One sign of spiritual maturity is being able to submit to others' advice. It's a biblical principle. We never want to get to the point where we think we know everything or are above receiving advice, direction, or correction. That applies to every Christian, for Ephesians 5:21 tells us to "submit to one another out of reverence for Christ" (NIV).

Submission is not bad news; it's good news! It's a place of safety and balance.

Hebrews 13:17 takes this one step further when talking about our submitting to pastors and those in spiritual leadership over us. It says to "obey those who rule over you, and be submissive, for they watch out for your souls, as those who must give account. Let them do so with joy and not with grief, for that would be unprofitable for you."

A lot of words in that verse are socially unacceptable in our world today—such words as "obey" and "rule over you" and "be submissive." But it's the Bible—it's God's truth—which means it's for your benefit.

> We never want to get to the point where we are above receiving advice, direction, or correction.

Notice the verse says your spiritual leaders "must give account" for your soul. That doesn't mean they are dictators over you or should make every decision for you. They are not meant to rule over every area of your life—or abuse you in any way. It just means that God has placed them in your life like a shepherd, to help and guide you. So don't be too proud to ask for and heed their advice.

Embrace Correction

It's also important to listen to your spiritual mentors and advisers when you need correction. Now, nobody likes to be corrected—even the Bible tells us that. It says, "No discipline is enjoyable while it is happening—it's painful!" (Heb. 12:11, NLT). Think about it: have you ever had a teacher or boss correct you? You might have felt embarrassed or humiliated or, at the very least, sheepish when they said, "You did that wrong."

It was painful! The Bible says it's normal to feel that way when you're corrected.

But if you were doing something wrong on a math problem or on the job, wasn't it good to be corrected so you could learn to do it *right*? If you aren't corrected for something you're doing wrong, you just keep doing it that way.

I don't want to keep doing something the wrong way. I want

to get it right. I don't want to keep going in the wrong direction, either. I want to go in the *right* direction in my life. To do that means learning to receive and act on correction.

Hebrews 12:11 goes on to say: "Nevertheless, afterward it [correction] yields the peaceable fruit of righteousness to those who have been trained by it." Correction is part of our training. Even though it's painful at the moment it's happening, it yields good fruit in our lives.

I've met so many Christians whose lives are going in the wrong direction, and they'll tell me about someone who tried to correct them—but they wouldn't listen. They seem surprised by how their life is going. Yet it's obvious to see that God sent people along the way to correct them. They just wouldn't listen. It's so important to be correctable.

When it comes to making decisions, sometimes you'll discover you've made the wrong one, and maybe one of your spiritual mentors or divinely placed friends will tell you so. When they do, I want to encourage you to receive their correction. In fact, do it gladly, because they're trying to help you go in the right direction!

The Merriam-Webster dictionary defines *correction* as "a change that makes something right, true, accurate, etc. The act of making something (such as an error or a bad condition) accurate or better." Learn to embrace correction so you can get better! Be ready to make a change that makes something right! That way you can turn around from a wrong decision and make a right one.

The Bible has a lot to say about correction. Proverbs 3:11–12 encourages you to avail yourself to it because God loves you and wants you to succeed: "My son [or daughter], do not despise the chastening of the LORD, nor detest His correction; for whom the LORD loves He corrects, just as a father the son [or daughter] in whom He delights." He delights in you, so He wants you going in the right direction.

Proverbs 10:17 says, "He who keeps instruction is in the way of life, but he who refuses correction goes astray." I don't know about you, but I don't want to go astray! So I must learn to receive and act on correction.

Proverbs 12:1 is one of the most pointed verses about correction. It says that "whoever loves instruction loves knowledge, but he who hates correction is stupid." Ouch! Let's not be stupid—let's embrace correction!

Proverbs 15:10 is more pointed still. It says, "He who hates correction will die." Wow, that's powerful. Don't let pride keep you from making corrections when needed.

Second Timothy 3:16–17 tells us that "all Scripture is given by inspiration of God, and is profitable for doctrine, for reproof, *for correction*, for instruction in righteousness, that the man of God may be complete, thoroughly equipped for every good work" (emphasis added). God wants you to be complete and equipped, and part of the way you get there is by being corrected.

Very often when we are corrected our flesh rises up. We want to defend ourselves. Pride can push its way to the forefront and we may think, "How dare they tell me that I'm wrong!" Sometimes it's hard to admit when we're wrong—or that we've made a decision that's taken us in a wrong direction. But isn't it worth the correction to be able to stop, turn, and go the other way? The alternative is ugly indeed: to keep going in the wrong direction just to save face. That won't get you where you want to go.

I've known people who made wrong decisions, but instead of turning around, they stubbornly sat in the wrong place rather than admit they were wrong. My spiritual father used to say,

"If you find yourself in the wrong place, turn around and go back to the last place you know God told you to be."

That can be taken literally or figuratively. But the most important thing is to *turn around*. Correct the wrong-direction course. Just admit you were wrong and go back.

The next time someone corrects you, remember these verses we've looked at and say, "Thank you." It takes some guts, but just determine in your heart that you will be easily corrected, that you will be someone who gets on board with the right direction *quickly*. Correction is a good thing. Let's learn how to become better and better at receiving it and acting on it.

REVIEW IN A NUTSHELL

God places people in our lives who can give us advice and wisdom that will be helpful when it comes to making decisions. It benefits us to listen, embrace correction, and submit ourselves to them.

NOW ENGAGE

Read and meditate on the scriptures we've looked at. Activate the power of God's Word in your life by speaking these declarations aloud:

> Where there is no counsel, the people fall; but in the multitude of counselors there is safety.
> —PROVERBS 11:14

DECLARE: "Father, thank You for those peers, mentors, and spiritual advisers You've put in my life to help me. I need them. I won't run away from them or ignore their advice. I will listen when they talk to me."

⁓⁓⁓

> A tree is known by its fruit.
> —MATTHEW 12:33

DECLARE: "My relationship with my mentor will be like the relationship Timothy had with the apostle Paul. I will be able to recognize a God-given mentor or spiritual adviser in my life by their fruit. They will have a good track record in their own walk with the Lord and visible results of good fruit in their life and ministry. In their interaction with me they will be encouraging but honest and comforting but challenging, and their main goal will be my growth and success. Father, thank

You for these kinds of relationships in my life. I will seek these people out and heed their advice!"

⁓⦵⦵⦵⦵

> By wise counsel you will wage your own war, and in a multitude of counselors there is safety.
>
> —PROVERBS 24:6

DECLARE: "I know I have to wage my own war and that no one else is going to do it for me. I know I am responsible to make my own decisions, with God's help. But I will also seek wisdom from my accountability partners and mentors. And when I do, I will ask their opinion, not just tell them mine. I will give them room to give me their opinion. I'll approach them with humility and a desire to hear what they have to say."

⁓⦵⦵⦵⦵

> Has the LORD indeed spoken only through Moses? Has He not spoken through us also?
>
> —NUMBERS 12:2

DECLARE: "I will not be too proud to seek advice or to listen and submit myself to others. I understand that there are times when good advice comes from those around me, and it will pay me rich dividends to heed it, even if I don't like the advice initially. I will be correctable and humbly receive good counsel."

⁓⦵⦵⦵⦵

> Obey those who rule over you, and be submissive, for they watch out for your souls, as those who must give

account. Let them do so with joy and not with grief, for that would be unprofitable for you.

—Hebrews 13:17

DECLARE: "I understand that I am accountable to my spiritual leadership, and I will submit accordingly because it's for my benefit."

⚬⚬⚬

Whoever loves instruction loves knowledge, but he who hates correction is stupid.

—Proverbs 12:1

DECLARE: "I know that correction is painful, but it's necessary for going in the right direction! I will learn to accept correction quickly and easily. I can admit when I'm wrong and turn around to go the right way."

KEY #6

TAP into the POWER

I HAVE EXCITING NEWS for you. You have a powerhouse inside you—the Holy Spirit! He came to live in you when you received Jesus as your Lord and Savior, as we already mentioned in Key #2. There are untold advantages to having the very Spirit of God living inside you. He can help you make the decisions of your life, and make sure you live in the fullness of God's covenant, free from the curse of the enemy.

> As born-again believers, we all have
> the Holy Spirit within us, and we all
> can also have the Holy Spirit upon us.

I love 1 John 4:4, which says, "Greater is he that is in you than he that is in the world" (KJV). The Holy Spirit in you is greater than any part of Satan's curse that comes against you in the world. He's greater than any sickness, fear, lack, or evil plot. The Greater One lives in you, with all His ability and power! In this chapter we're going to learn how to tap into that power to help us make decisions. We don't have to do any of this in our own natural strength or ability—He's helping us.

He Reveals Things to You

The Holy Spirit's main ministry to you and me, as believers, is revelation. He *reveals* the things of God—God's will—to us. As the apostle Paul writes in 1 Corinthians 2:9–10: "Eye has not seen, nor ear heard, nor have entered into the heart of man the things which God has prepared for those who love Him. But God has revealed them to us through His Spirit."

> There are untold advantages to having the very Spirit of God living inside you.

Notice this verse doesn't say, "Eye has not seen, ear has not heard, the things God has prepared—and you're never going to find out what they are!" No, Paul says God has made provision for you to know what God has prepared for you. He has *revealed them through His Spirit.* You and I are in God's inner circle. We are privy to inside information. By His Spirit He will reveal to you the things He's prepared for you.

The way He does this is either by enlightening God's Word to you as you read and meditate on it or by the inward witness, which we talked about in Key #2. This is how He can reveal things to you when you're making a decision, such as where to live, where to work, whom to marry, and so on. He knows these things, and He wants to pass them on to you to help you make the right decisions in your life.

The apostle Paul goes on to say:

> For the Spirit searches all things, yes, the deep things of God. For what man knows the things of a man except the spirit of the man which is in him? Even so no one knows the things of God except the Spirit of God. Now we have

received, not the spirit of the world, but the Spirit who is
from God, that we might know the things that have been
freely given to us by God.
—1 CORINTHIANS 2:10–12

You have received the gift of the Holy Spirit because God
wants you to have, know, and operate in everything that your
covenant says is yours—everything Jesus died to give you. He
wants you to know all that He's prepared for your life. He's not
holding anything back from you!

The Baptism of the Holy Spirit

Proverbs 20:5 says, "Counsel in the heart of man is like deep
water, but a man of understanding will draw it out." There is
a way to draw out that counsel—those "deep things of God"
referred to in 1 Corinthians 2:10—from our inward man (our
heart). It's called the baptism of the Holy Spirit.

You see, in addition to the Holy Spirit coming to live inside
you (known as the indwelling of the Holy Spirit), there is a
subsequent experience available for all Christians. It is the
baptism of the Holy Spirit. This gift is the main thing Jesus
wanted His disciples to know about when He reappeared to
them after dying on the cross.

Before He ascended to heaven, Jesus told them to go to Jerusalem and wait for this endowment of power. He said, "John
truly baptized with water, but you shall be baptized with the
Holy Spirit not many days from now" (Acts 1:5). Then He went
on to say, "You shall receive power when the Holy Spirit has
come *upon* you" (v. 8, emphasis added).

As born-again believers, we all have the Holy Spirit within us,
and we all can also have the Holy Spirit upon us, just as Jesus
told His disciples. We can have this power Jesus talked about!

The disciples followed His instructions and went to wait in

Jerusalem, where the Bible says they all were together in the Upper Room when something amazing happened:

> When the Day of Pentecost had fully come, they were all with one accord in one place. And suddenly there came a sound from heaven, as of a rushing mighty wind, and it filled the whole house where they were sitting. Then there appeared to them divided tongues, as of fire, and one sat upon each of them. And they were all filled with the Holy Spirit and began to speak with other tongues, as the Spirit gave them utterance.
>
> —ACTS 2:1–4

As we can see from these verses, the evidence of receiving this endowment of power, or the Holy Spirit coming *upon* us, is speaking with other tongues. Speaking in tongues is simply speaking in a language that only God understands. This is not some sort of weird manifestation of cultish zealots. It is the evidence of the power that God has entrusted us with. It is a *good gift*!

Speaking in tongues is tapping
into the power of God.

And it is full of power, which is what we need in this life, especially if we're facing decisions. We can see that after being filled (or baptized) with the Holy Spirit, the disciples' lives were never the same again. Look at Peter, for example. He had just denied Jesus three times (Matt. 26:74–75), an act that could have completely derailed him with guilt and remorse.

After Jesus died, I'm sure Peter was feeling terrible about denying his Lord, and the devil was probably hounding him about how unfit he was for ministry. But look what happened right after Peter was filled with the Holy Spirit and spoke with other tongues on the Day of Pentecost. Acts 2:14–40 tells us he preached a powerful sermon and that, as a result, about three thousand people in one day were saved and baptized!

Being filled with the Holy Spirit changed Peter from a man who was ashamed to acknowledge Jesus (and probably feeling horribly guilty for it) into a bold preacher who talked about Jesus on the streets of Jerusalem without fear. And talk about powerful results! At least three thousand people got saved that day. I don't know about you, but that's power I need. Speaking in tongues is tapping into the power of God.

Get Charged Up

The Book of Acts records five examples of believers receiving the baptism of the Holy Spirit: Acts 2:1–4; 8:5–18; 9:10–12, 17–18; 10:34–48; 19:1–6. Then throughout the rest of the New Testament there are examples of the wonderful benefits of speaking in other tongues—benefits that belong to you and me today.

One of those benefits is *edification.* The Greek word translated *edify* includes the meaning "to charge"—in the sense of recharging a battery. It's like recharging your cell phone when it runs out of juice: when your phone battery dies, you can't make a call until you recharge it.

In the human sense, you and I know what it feels like to run out of juice. We can get tired and run down, physically, mentally, emotionally, and spiritually. We can get so busy or have so many negative things going on around us that we can get overwhelmed. We can lose sight of God and our purpose in Him and succumb to the flesh at every turn.

But the Bible says in the Book of Jude that there's a cure for that, a way to get charged up again:

> In the last time there will be mockers, following after their own ungodly lusts…devoid of the Spirit. But you, beloved, building yourselves up on your most holy faith, praying in the Holy Spirit, keep yourselves in the love of God.
>
> —Jude 18–21, NAS

You and I can build ourselves up—recharge—by praying in the Holy Spirit, or praying in other tongues. What a great benefit that is! Notice it also helps us to keep ourselves in the love of God, which is the only new commandment the Lord gave us in the New Testament. (See John 13:34–35.) When you're too worn out in your heart and mind to make the right decision, you can pray in tongues and recharge your spiritual battery. That sets you in place again to hear the leading of God much more clearly.

First Corinthians 14:4 gives further credence to this idea of getting recharged or edified. It says, "He who speaks in a tongue edifies himself." Thank God that there is a way we can recharge when we're facing a decision but have run out of our own power. We can tap into all of God's power, strength, peace, joy, and rest by praying in other tongues.

Every time I've faced a major decision in life, I've taken extra time to pray in tongues. I'll get in the car and take a long drive, speaking in tongues the whole time. It helps my spirit to be more perceptive and sensitive to the things of God's Spirit and to hear the Lord's voice more clearly.

When I pray with people to receive the baptism of the Holy Spirit, I often tell them to "practice" by praying every night before they go to sleep. I say: "As soon as your head hits the pillow, start speaking in tongues, and you'll fall asleep doing it. This is a great habit to start. And when you wake up, you'll know things!"

To understand and tap into spiritual things we must exercise our spirit, or charge it up. Praying in other tongues helps you tap into all of God's power. It's vital for helping you make the right decisions in your life.

Speak Right to God

Another benefit of speaking in tongues is that no one understands it except God. You're talking right to Him when you speak in other tongues. Nothing is intercepting or scrambling the conversation. The apostle Paul writes in 1 Corinthians 14:2: "For he who speaks in a tongue does not speak to men but to God, for no one understands him; however, in the spirit he speaks mysteries."

> You and I can build ourselves up—recharge—by praying in the Holy Spirit, or praying in other tongues.

Listen, the future is a mystery to us. If you're trying to make a decision, the outcome of that decision is still a mystery to you, right? But when you pray in tongues, you're talking right to God, and He knows the future. You're praying out the mysteries. I fully believe that when we pray in tongues, we're praying out the future, so that by the time we get there many things have already been set straight and taken care of in the spirit realm.

When you speak right to God in tongues, whatever you're saying bypasses your mind so that any incorrect natural thinking you may have won't get in the way. Paul explains this further in 1 Corinthians 14:14: "If I pray in a tongue, my spirit prays, but my understanding is unfruitful." That can be a great help if your mind is running in circles or giving you fits about all the possible consequences of your decision.

Praying in tongues can quiet your mind down so you can come to a place of peace, where it's much easier for you to hear the voice of God. You're praying with your spirit (the born-again part of you that's just like God)—not with your own natural thinking and understanding.

> When we pray in the Spirit, we're letting Him pray for the perfect outcome of any situation.

Another benefit is that the devil can't understand tongues either! So there's no place for him to get a foothold or to try and stop the plan. Praying in tongues is like your special hotline to God. No one else can tap into it. It's your spirit praying directly to His Spirit and getting all the help you need to make the right decisions.

When You Don't Know What to Pray

Another benefit of praying in other tongues is found in Romans 8:26, which says, "The Spirit also helps in our weaknesses. For we do not know what we should pray for as we ought, but the Spirit Himself makes intercession for us with groanings which cannot be uttered."

Have you ever been in a situation where you didn't know what to pray? I sure have! Thankfully God has that covered too. This verse shows us that praying in tongues helps us to pray when we do not know what or how to pray.

You and I have limited knowledge about what's going on all around us. We have limited knowledge of what's going on in the spirit realm, or in the future. But the Holy Spirit has all knowledge about it. When we pray in the Spirit, we're letting Him pray for the perfect outcome of any situation. We're praying His perfect will. What a blessing!

You may also be familiar with the scripture two verses after this one, Romans 8:28, which says, "And we know that all things work together for good to those who love God, to those who are the called according to His purpose." I believe Romans 8:26 and 28 go together. First you pray in the Spirit (in other tongues), and as a result God can work all things together for your good. Another way of saying it is: God can cause all things to work together for your good when you pray in the Spirit.

Many times I find myself in situations where I don't know what to pray for, especially when other people are involved. Most of the time when I'm helping other people, all sorts of dynamics are going on behind the scenes in their lives that I don't know anything about. They'll usually tell me their version of what's happening, or what they think needs to happen, but there's always more than one side to every story.

So I pray in the Spirit—I tap into the power of God—because the Word tells me to when I don't know what to pray for. Sometimes when I do that, I'll eventually get a peace in my spirit that lets me know I've prayed through to the answer, even though I may never know what the answer is.

For example, I've had God wake me up in the night with an urgency to pray. I might get an impression that it's for one of my missionary friends or a family member or something coming up. Sometimes I won't know what it's about at all. And since I don't know exactly *what* I'm praying for, I'll pray in tongues. After a while, maybe an hour or two or sometimes longer, the urgency will lift and I'll know the problem has been taken care of.

At other times the problem will be something that's going on in my own life, but I don't have the answer or direction for it. Since I don't know really *what* to pray for, I'll make a point to pray in tongues all through the day, whenever I think about that need. Usually within a day or two, sometimes sooner, I'll know what to do. Praying in the Spirit helps me make the right decisions.

It's no wonder that 2 Peter 1:3 says, "By his divine power, God has given us everything we need for living a godly life" (NLT). Among His many other blessings, God has given us the baptism of the Holy Spirit!

> Praying in the Spirit helps me
> make the right decisions.

Supernatural Boldness

Another benefit of speaking in tongues is that it will help you to be bold. When Jesus commanded His disciples to go to Jerusalem and wait for the endowment of Holy Spirit power, He told them it would give them the power to be His witnesses "in Jerusalem, and in all Judea and Samaria, and to the end of the earth" (Acts 1:8).

Now I don't know about you, but I used to be less than bold when it came to witnessing. Telling someone about Jesus made me very nervous. I did *not* have the power to be a witness, neither in Jerusalem nor in all Judea and Samaria—or even in my neighborhood grocery store!

One time years ago I was in a grocery store near Christmastime, and in the vegetable section I saw a woman who was wearing an oxygen mask and carrying an oxygen tank in her shopping cart. I felt like the Lord spoke to me and said, "Go pray for her." I was immediately nervous. I silently argued with God, "What if she doesn't believe in healing? What if she doesn't want to be prayed for? What if someone sees me?" and on and on. Obviously I wasn't thinking about the woman at all, only about myself.

Finally I said, "OK, Lord, if I see her in the next aisle over, I'll pray for her." I went on my way, and guess who I met in the next aisle? You guessed it. And I again prayed, "But Lord, what if I pray and she doesn't get healed? What if I embarrass her?" as if I was really worried about *her* being embarrassed. Finally I said, "OK, Lord, if I see her in the bread aisle I'll pray for her." I'm sure you can guess what happened.

To make a long story short, I had the same argument with God, made the same deal, saw her in *every* aisle, and *still* didn't pray for. Then I ended up in the checkout line right behind her! And I *still* didn't pray for her. You can plainly see that I was not bold.

As it turned out, I was walking through the parking lot to my car and saw the woman putting groceries in her trunk when the Lord finally said to me, "Karen, are you going to let her spend Christmas without being able to breathe?" Well, that did it. I walked up to her, asked if I could pray for her, and she said, "Oh, yes, please!" So I prayed for her and she was grateful. I felt the healing power of God go out of me into her, and I just believe she went home and was able to breathe better than she had in a long time. The moral of the story is: I was a chicken when it came to stepping out and witnessing or praying for people.

But after I was baptized in the Holy Spirit and began to speak with other tongues, I got bolder! Now when the Holy Spirit gently nudges me to pray for someone or witness to them, the compassion of Jesus rises up in me and I do it right away. Now it's about *them*, not about me. Being baptized with the Holy Spirit has given me a boldness. And in fact, I have gotten bolder about a lot of things, including decision making. I have an inward confidence that helps me in every area of life.

If there was ever a time when we Christians need boldness in every area of our lives, it's now—in the last days. You and I have a job to do, a purpose to fulfill in the earth today, and we're going to need all the boldness we can use. We're going to need a holy boldness to make the right decisions in our lives. Aren't you thankful that God put His Spirit right inside us to help us be bold?

I like what one minister says: "Praying in the Spirit will take the chicken out of you." In other words, it will make you less afraid—it will make you bold. When it comes to making decisions, you don't want to be chicken; you want to be bold. That holy boldness is what happened to Peter on the day of Pentecost, and that's what can happen to you too!

How to Receive

If you already speak in tongues, I encourage you to do it more—for all the reasons above. The apostle Paul said, "I thank my God I speak with tongues more than you all" (1 Cor. 14:18). I like the word *more* in that verse! Do you suppose there's a connection between Paul's praying in tongues more than everyone else and the fact that he was the greatest apostle of his day? I think the two are related, for sure. I also think that praying in the Spirit helped Paul when he was making life-and-death decisions about where to preach, whom to preach to, and so on. Paul knew how to tap into the power, and we can do it too. We should pray in tongues *more*!

But if you've never spoken in tongues and received this

endowment of power, it's high time you did. It's not hard, and you don't have to qualify for it or earn it. Speaking in tongues is a free gift from God for all His children. He wants you to have it.

If there was ever a time when we
Christians need boldness in every area
of our lives, it's now—in the last days.

If I were to walk up to you with a gift in my hands and say, "This is for you," what would you have to do to receive it? Would you have to pay me for it? Would you have to perform or beg in order to receive it? No. I said it was a gift for you. All you would need to do would be to reach out and take it, wouldn't you? That's all you have to do with this gift from God too.

First, to be filled with the Holy Spirit, you must be born again:

> Then Peter said to them, "Repent, and let every one of you
> be baptized in the name of Jesus Christ for the remission
> of sins; and you shall receive the gift of the Holy Spirit.
> For the promise is to you and to your children, and to all
> who are afar off, as many as the Lord our God will call."
> —ACTS 2:38–39

If you are not sure if you're born again, read "Your Most Important Decision" at the end of the book, and then come back here and keep reading.

The baptism of the Holy Spirit is received by faith, just as the new birth is received by faith. Jesus said in Luke 11:13, "If you then, being evil, know how to give good gifts to your children, how much more will your heavenly Father give the Holy Spirit to those who ask Him!" When you ask in faith, the Holy Spirit comes upon you, and you'll speak in tongues. It's as simple as that.

Notice I said it's *you* who will speak in tongues. It will be your tongue, your breath, and your vocal cords doing the talking. Simply yield your tongue to His use. You'll supply the sounds, and the Holy Spirit will supply the words. You'll be forming syllables around the expression that your heart desires to release. Speaking words unknown to you might seem awkward at first, but just keep practicing like a child learning to speak.

> The baptism of the Holy Spirit
> is received by faith, just as the
> new birth is received by faith.

To receive the baptism in the Holy Spirit you don't need to "get a word from God" about it—you already have His Word. You don't need to wait. The only waiting was done on the Day of Pentecost. The Holy Spirit came to Earth that day, and He's been here ever since.

And you don't need to worry about being deceived and ending up with something that is from the devil. When you ask your heavenly Father for one of His promises, such as the baptism in the Holy Spirit, you can be confident the gift given is from God, not Satan.

If you're ready, just ask God right now. You could pray something like this:

Father, I'm a believer. Your Word says if I'll ask, I'll receive the Holy Spirit. So in the name of Jesus, I'm asking You to baptize me in the Holy Spirit. Because of Your Word, I believe that I receive. Thank You! Now, Holy Spirit, rise up within me as I praise God. I fully expect to speak with other tongues, as You give me the utterance.

Now begin to speak, giving voice to the expressions that rise up from your inner man. Speak and hear the Holy Spirit speaking through you. Praise God! You've just been baptized in the Holy Spirit, endowed with your heavenly Father's power. Now keep on speaking, and keep on practicing.

Keep on tapping into the power!

REVIEW IN A NUTSHELL

We can tap into the power of God by praying in the Spirit. There are many benefits to praying in other tongues, including insight and boldness to make the right decisions.

NOW ENGAGE

Read and meditate on the scriptures we've looked at. Activate the power of God's Word in your life by speaking these declarations aloud:

> Greater is He who is in you than he who is in the world.
> —1 John 4:4, nas

DECLARE: "I have a powerhouse inside me—the Holy Spirit! He can help me in making the decisions of my life. The Holy Spirit in me is greater than any part of Satan's curse that comes against me in the world. He's greater than any sickness, fear, lack, or evil plot. The Greater One lives in me, with all His ability and power!"

⸎

> Eye has not seen, nor ear heard, nor have entered into the heart of man the things which God has prepared for those who love Him. But God has revealed them to us through His Spirit.
> —1 Corinthians 2:9–10

DECLARE: "God has made provision for me to know what He has prepared for me—He has revealed it through His Spirit. I'm in God's inner circle, privy to inside information. His Spirit reveals it to me as I read and meditate on His Word, as well as by the inward witness. God wants me to know all that He's prepared for my life. He's not holding anything back from me!"

∽∾∽

> But you, beloved, building yourselves up on your most holy faith, praying in the Holy Spirit, keep yourselves in the love of God.
> —JUDE 20–21, NAS

DECLARE: "I can keep myself in the love of God and build myself up—recharge—by praying in other tongues. If I'm too tired in my own strength to make the right decisions, I can pray in tongues and recharge my spiritual battery. That sets me in place to hear the leading of God much more clearly."

∽∾∽

> For he who speaks in a tongue does not speak to men but to God, for no one understands him; however, in the spirit he speaks mysteries.
> —1 CORINTHIANS 14:2

DECLARE: "The future is a mystery to me. When I pray in tongues, I'm talking right to God. I'm praying out the mysteries of the future, so that by the time I get there many things will have already been taken care of in the spirit realm."

∽∾∽

> For if I pray in a tongue, my spirit prays, but my understanding is unfruitful.
> —1 CORINTHIANS 14:14

DECLARE: "When I speak right to God in tongues, whatever I'm saying bypasses my mind so that any incorrect natural thinking won't get in the way. It stops my mind from running in circles so it's easier for me to hear the voice of God. The devil can't understand tongues either, so there's no place for him to get a foothold or to try and stop the plan. Praying in tongues is like my special hotline to God. It's my spirit praying directly to His Spirit and getting all the help I need to make the right decisions."

∽∽∽

The Spirit also helps in our weaknesses. For we do not know what we should pray for as we ought, but the Spirit Himself makes intercession for us with groanings which cannot be uttered.

—Romans 8:26

DECLARE: "When I don't know what or how to pray, the Holy Spirit helps me—I can pray in tongues. I have limited knowledge about what's really going on, but the Holy Spirit has all knowledge about it. When I pray in the Spirit, I'm letting Him pray for the perfect outcome of any situation. I'm praying His perfect will."

∽∽∽

But you shall receive power when the Holy Spirit has come upon you; and you shall be witnesses to Me in Jerusalem, and in all Judea and Samaria, and to the end of the earth.

—Acts 1:8

DECLARE: "As I pray more and more in tongues, the Bible says I'll get bolder about a lot of things, including making decisions. I'll get an inward confidence that helps me in every area of life. I have a job to do, a purpose to fulfill in the earth today, and praying in tongues will take the chicken out of me!"

KEY #7

DO WHAT JESUS DID

I F THERE IS any life that you and I should follow as our example, it's Jesus's life. One of the reasons He became flesh and dwelt among us as a person was so He could understand what we go through and show us how to live. Hebrews 4:15 says, "For we do not have a High Priest who cannot sympathize with our weaknesses, but was in all points tempted as we are, yet without sin." Jesus understands completely what it is to be human.

> When we're facing decisions, there is
> no better prayer to pray than, "Not
> my will, but Your will be done."

We all have heroes in this life, both spiritual and natural heroes, whom we try to emulate and imitate. But if we just imitate Jesus and use Him as our constant example, even in decision making, we will always overcome. If, in every situation, we asked ourselves, "What would Jesus do?", we'd always end up with the right answer, wouldn't we? He is our best example.

So what did Jesus do when He was facing a major decision?

He got completely honest with His Father and consecrated Himself. He prayed a prayer of dedication and submission to the will of God.

God's Will Be Done

The biggest decision Jesus ever faced in His life here was in the Garden of Gethsemane. As His final hours of life drew near, the Bible tells us that Jesus was sorrowful and heavy (Matt. 26:38; Mark 14:34). Even though He had known all along that He came to pay the ultimate price and die for the sins of the world, He was, after all, human. He battled the temptation to draw back from what was to come because it was horrible and repulsive to His flesh.

On that terrible night before His crucifixion He prayed to God: "Father, if it is Your will, take this cup away from Me; nevertheless not My will, but Yours, be done" (Luke 22:42). The Bible says He sweated drops of blood as He wrestled. It wasn't easy for Him to fulfill the Father's plan.

But Jesus knew the outcome of redemption would be the salvation of mankind, so for the joy set before Him, He surrendered to His Father's will (Heb. 12:2). That night Jesus set an example for us and prayed a prayer of consecration and dedication: "O My Father, if this cup cannot pass away from Me unless I drink it, *Your will be done*" (Matt. 26:42, emphasis added).

He consecrated Himself to do the will of God regardless of His personal feelings or desires. He wanted to do what the Father wanted Him to do. If Jesus needed to consecrate Himself to do the will of God, then we need to consecrate ourselves too! We all want God's best for our lives, but we qualify for His best only when we choose to obey Him and submit our wills to His.

God is looking for believers who will dedicate and consecrate themselves to carry out His plan for their lives, just as Jesus did at Gethsemane and throughout His earthly ministry. Second Chronicles 16:9 says the Lord's eyes roam throughout the earth to find people whose hearts are dedicated to Him. God is looking for believers who will say, as Jesus did, "Not *my* will, Father, but *Your* will be done."

Sometimes we ask God for direction,
but we have little caveats that prevent
Him from bringing His plan to pass.

When we pray the prayer of consecration, we are dedicating our whole being to do the will of God. The prayer of consecration causes us to flow into the purposes of God for our lives. It brings us into harmony with God's highest call for our lives. Instead of asking God to bless our plans, we are choosing through consecration to find out what His best is for our lives, and we are committing to follow Him fully.

One definition of the verb *consecrate* is "to devote to a purpose." I think you'll agree that Jesus was completely devoted to His purpose. He put His own wishes and feelings aside in order to fulfill God's plan of redemption. He gave His own life to purchase your life and mine. That's why we call His crucifixion "the passion of Christ." It was with passion, or strong emotion and zeal, that He completed His mission on the earth.

But He did it by laying down His own will in favor of the Father's. When we're facing decisions and seeking God's will for our lives, there is no better prayer to pray than, "Not my will, but Your will be done." It is the prayer that never fails.

The Only Place

It must be mentioned here that in the prayer of consecration, the phrase, "If it be Your will," is a good thing. But don't get confused—when it comes to praying *a prayer of faith*, or petition, we don't pray, "If it be Your will." The prayer of faith is the prayer to change things, and we pray it according to God's Word.

In other words, we can pray in faith to receive healing because we know the Bible says, "By [His] stripes you were healed" (1 Pet. 2:24). We don't pray, "If it be Your will to heal me," because we *know* His will in that case is healing. He said so in His Word. When it comes to changing things or receiving something God has promised us in our covenant, we don't pray, "If it be Your will," because we already have God's Word concerning it.

For example, if you're asking God to meet a financial need, you don't pray, "Father, if it be Your will, please meet my need." No, He said in Philippians 4:19 that He supplies all your needs according to His riches in glory by Christ Jesus. So you have His Word on it. You already *know* it's His will. His Word is His will.

If you prayed, "If it be Your will," for something already provided in Christ (such as healing or provision), you would be praying in doubt. "If" is the badge of doubt when it comes to praying in faith. The only place we pray, "If it be Your will," is in this prayer of consecration.

Get Willing

When it comes to making decisions, sometimes we have an inkling of what God wants us to do—or part of the plan is clear, but other parts are not. Over and over again I've seen someone ask God for direction, get an understanding of the plan, and use their faith to receive it or walk it out—but also have certain areas where they are hanging back. They have conditional limitations that they themselves have set. In other words, there are places in their heart where they aren't willing.

For example, I know one gentleman who wanted to get married. He was in his forties and had been divorced for years, and he had come to the place where he just didn't want to spend the rest of his life alone. He'd prayed about it and asked God for a nice Christian woman to marry, but nothing had happened. It turns out that he had put a *condition* on his prayer. He had said, "Lord, I don't want to marry anyone who has children." Time went by, and he remained unmarried.

> I know from experience that God will
> provide grace in every situation of
> life if we're willing to follow Him.

Then one day after spending some time in the Word and prayer, he was getting ready for work and the thought suddenly dropped into his spirit that he wouldn't mind having stepchildren. So he said, "OK, Lord, I would marry someone who has children." It was only two or three weeks later that he met a woman at his gym who had two children. He liked her, they started dating, and they were married within the year.

I think that sometimes when we ask God for direction, we have little caveats that prevent Him from bringing His plan to pass. I've known people, and you have too, who have said, "Yes, I'll follow God's plan, but I'll never...move away; marry a preacher; go back there; spend that much; buy a Mac; own a car like that; or [insert your own phrase here]."

Sometimes when we say "never" like that, we're looking at the decision from outside the grace that would enable us to do it. I like to call grace, "God's power beyond our ability." If we were to step outside those boundaries we've set and end up doing something we said we'd never do, we would find that God gives us the grace—His power beyond our ability—to do it—just as He gave Jesus the power beyond human ability (grace) to go to the cross and bear our sin.

You Have Grace

I know from experience that God will provide grace in every situation of life if we're willing to follow Him. When my first husband died and I had to take over pastoring our church and raising our teenage sons by myself, many other pastors' wives looked at me and said, "I could never do it!" But I always told them, "You could if God told you to, because He gives the grace."

God provides grace for all of us, for whatever we're going through.

They were looking at the situation from outside the grace, so it looked impossible. Have you ever seen someone going through a trial with a smile or someone who lives a pressure-filled life and thought, "How are they doing that? I could never do it!" Well, that's because you don't have the grace for it—it's not your life. You're looking at it from outside the grace. *They* have a grace to live their life, even in the hard times.

That's great news. It means that when it *is* your life, you can expect to have the grace for it. No matter what happens in your life, God gives you grace for it. So you don't ever have to be afraid of whether or not you can handle a certain situation—when you find yourself in it, then there will be grace to handle it. Don't worry if you think you won't be able to handle it right *now*. You're not in that situation right now! Just believe and know that God will be there with His grace when you need it.

It took me a while to figure that out. For example, I didn't really like being a pastor's wife. I complained about it and had wrong thinking about it. I saw myself as "less than" others, and as a result, I was tormented by feelings of inferiority. Then, after my first husband died and I became the pastor, I felt the grace to do it—it was almost a tangible thing.

And I realized: "You know what? I have a feeling that the grace to be a pastor's wife was always available for me too, but I fought it. I complained and thought wrongly about it." That's when I realized that God provides grace for all of us, for whatever we're going through.

The apostle Paul said it this way: "I do not treat the grace of God as meaningless" (Gal. 2:21, NLT). God has given His grace to you for every situation of life. It's not your power and ability; it's His. You have grace to be you! Don't resist it as I did. Instead, look for the grace. Expect it. Say, "Father, this is hard, but I know You have provided grace for me in this situation. I embrace Your grace!"

Thank goodness, you and I aren't the captains of our own ships. First Corinthians 6:19–20 says, "Do you now know…you are not your own? For you were bought at a price." When you said yes to Jesus as your Lord, you turned the helm of your life over to Him. You aren't facing anything alone; He's giving you His grace and wisdom in every situation.

That also means you gave up the right to direct your own life. Jesus is supposed to be directing it! And that's how it should be. He knows everything and He loves you. Who better to be the captain of your ship? Don't fight Him; He knows the way. And don't put conditional limitations on your willingness. He didn't. There were no limitations on His willingness to die for you and me. He didn't say, "I'd never die a criminal's death on the cross for something I didn't do." No, He consecrated Himself to do the Father's plan, not His own. And He had the grace to do it.

> When you're making a decision,
> be sure to do what Jesus did:
> consecrate yourself to God.

If you feel the Lord tugging you to do something that you haven't accepted before, don't resist Him. Isaiah 1:19 says, "If you are willing and obedient, you shall eat the good of the land." It takes both obedience *and* willingness to walk in God's plan for your life. He will lead you into something that will render *only* tremendous benefits! His plans for you are *good*, remember? You can trust Him! Search your heart and be sure that you are willing. God's instructions to the Israelites still stand as His instructions for you today:

> See, I have set before you today life and good, death and evil, in that I command you today to love the LORD your God, to walk in His ways, and to keep His commandments, His statutes, and His judgments, that you may live and multiply; and the LORD your God will bless you in the land which you go to possess....I call heaven and earth as witnesses today against you, that I have set before you life and death, blessing and cursing;

therefore choose life, that both you and your descendants may live.

—DEUTERONOMY 30:15–16, 19

Trust that God's plan is best. We read in Hebrews 12:2 that Jesus went to the cross "for the joy that was set before Him" He knew the result of obeying God would be joyful. The same is true for you! You can trust when you pray, "Father, Your will be done," His will is *good* and that when you obey Him, when you lay aside your will for His, your results will also be joyful.

Maybe there will be some sacrifices along the way, and maybe your flesh draws back from the thought of that, but obeying God always turns out in the end to be the best thing for *you*. When you're making a decision, be sure to do what Jesus did: consecrate yourself to God. He has the best in store for you.

REVIEW IN A NUTSHELL

When we're making decisions in our lives, we need to be sure we have consecrated ourselves to God—that we are laying down our will for His. His best comes to us when we obey Him.

NOW ENGAGE

Read and meditate on the scriptures we've looked at. Activate the power of God's Word in your life by speaking these declarations aloud:

> For we do not have a High Priest who cannot sympathize with our weaknesses, but was in all points tempted as we are, yet without sin.
> —HEBREWS 4:15

DECLARE: "Jesus understands completely what it is to be human. He is my example. If I imitate and emulate Him, I will always overcome. For the joy set before Him, He prayed the prayer of consecration, and I can too. Father, *Your will be done.*"

⸱⸱⸱⸱⸱

> Father, if it is Your will, take this cup away from Me; nevertheless not My will, but Yours, be done.
> —LUKE 22:42

DECLARE: "Jesus consecrated Himself to do the will of God, regardless of His personal feelings or desires. He wanted to do what the Father wanted Him to do, and I do too. If Jesus needed to consecrate Himself to do the will of God, then I do too, and I do it willingly. As I obey Him and submit my will to His, I qualify for His best."

❧

The eyes of the Lord run to and fro throughout the whole earth, to show Himself strong on behalf of those whose heart is loyal to Him.
—2 CHRONICLES 16:9

DECLARE: "God is looking for believers who will say, as Jesus did, 'Not *my* will, Father, but *Your* will be done.' Here I am, Father! My heart is dedicated to You. I dedicate my whole being to do Your will. As a result, I will flow into Your purposes. I am in harmony with Your highest call for my life. I am committed to following You fully."

❧

I do not treat the grace of God as meaningless.
—GALATIANS 2:21, NLT

DECLARE: "God gives His grace to me for every situation in my life. It's not my power and ability that I need; it's His. I have grace to be me! I'm not going to resist it. I'm going to look for it and expect it. I embrace God's grace."

❧

Do you not know…you are not your own? For you were bought at a price.
—1 CORINTHIANS 6:19–20

DECLARE: "I am not the captain of my own ship. When I said yes to Jesus as my Lord, I turned the helm of my life over to Him, and I gave up the right to direct it on my own. I won't put conditional limitations on my willingness. There were no limitations on His willingness to die for me. I will consecrate myself, just as Jesus consecrated Himself."

———

If you are willing and obedient, you shall eat the good of the land.

—Isaiah 1:19

DECLARE: "When I feel the Lord tugging me to do something that I haven't accepted before, I won't resist Him—I'll get willing and I'll obey. I believe He will lead me into something that will render only tremendous benefits. His plans for me are good, and I trust Him."

KEY #8

GET BACK on TRACK

SOMETIMES WHEN PEOPLE come to me about making right decisions in their lives, I find that they've made a wrong decision somewhere along the way. They are beating themselves up over it, afraid of trying again. Or there are others who are so scared of making a mistake—for fear of getting "out of God's will"—that they're paralyzed in their decision-making process. They're too afraid of missing it to make any decision at all, so they just don't make one. They've gotten off track with God's plan for their lives simply because they haven't decided *anything*, one way or the other. They're stuck in indecision.

If either of those people sounds like you, I want you to know there's good news for you. God wants to get you back on track! And He knows just how to do it.

Let's talk first about the fear of making a mistake and how to get back on track. Then we'll get to the issue of what to do if you've already made a wrong decision.

Fear of Deciding

There was a time in my life when I was afraid of making the wrong decision. I mentioned this before in Key #1 when I was talking about not making a pro-con list to decide about moving back to Tulsa, Oklahoma. The year was 2000, and I had been pastoring our church in Boise, Idaho, for about four years since my first husband (the founding pastor) had died. I felt like the Lord was leading me to turn the church over to my associate pastor and move back to Tulsa. But I was scared.

It was a huge decision to make all on my own. Taking over the church sort of just happened *to* me. It was kind of an automatic thing. I didn't exactly choose it; I just took it on.

But this—choosing to uproot my teenage sons, turn over my church, sell my house, and move halfway across the country—was my decision alone. I got lots of advice from mentors and close friends and I prayed about it a great deal, but in the end I was the one who had to decide. I felt the terrible pressure of that decision.

At one point I just became paralyzed. I was so scared of "missing it," of making a mistake and getting out of God's will. What if moving away was the wrong choice? It wasn't just my life that would be affected, but also the lives of my children, my congregation, my extended family, and who knows how many other people.

One night while I was agonizing over whether or not to pull the trigger on this whole move, I felt like the Lord said to me, "Karen, even if you were missing it by moving to Tulsa, I'm big enough to get you back on track."

Wow! That set me free! It made me realize that if I just kept my heart right, seeking His will and not being rebellious or prideful, God would know where I was the whole time. And if I was in the wrong place, He was big enough to rectify the situation. I knew then He is just looking for willing and obedient hearts and that the rest is up to Him. If you miss it, God still knows the way back and just how to get you there. You're never outside His tender loving care of you. The psalmist said it like this:

Where can I go from Your Spirit? Or where can I flee from Your presence? If I ascend into heaven, You are there; If I make my bed in hell, behold, You are there. If I take the wings of the morning, and dwell in the uttermost parts of the sea, even there Your hand shall lead me, and Your right hand shall hold me.

—PSALM 139:7–10

In the New Testament Jesus said it this way: "What man of you, having a hundred sheep, if he loses one of them, does not leave the ninety-nine in the wilderness, and go after the one which is lost until he finds it?" (Luke 15:4).

God is big enough to get
you back on track!

Trust me, if you wander off track, Your heavenly Father wants to come after you and bring you back. If your heart's cry is, "Father, I just want to hear You and do Your will," know that He's standing by to help. He can do anything with a heart like that. It's when you set yourself against Him that you're in trouble (more about that coming up). Otherwise, He's available to rescue you and get you back on track. I love that about Him.

We've all "missed it" at one time or another. There have been times when I thought I'd heard from God, taken steps in a particular direction, and then found out the direction I was taking was wrong. So what? God was big enough to get me back on track! He just wants us to be willing to listen and step out in faith, holding fast to Him.

A New Perspective

I once talked to a woman—let's call her Sheri—who just couldn't make a certain major decision in her life. She was stuck in indecision, and because of it she was miserable. Sheri had been married to her husband for more than thirty years. It was a second marriage for both of them. Her first marriage had ended after thirteen years when her husband left her for another woman.

Sheri told me that she had had maybe two or three good years in this second marriage. The rest of them were awful. She didn't tell me all the details, but she said, "I have every biblical reason to divorce him, but I've tried to hang on, hoping for a change. I've spent most of these thirty-plus years trying to decide to stay or go."

Only a couple of close Christian friends knew about her situation and, trying to help, they would tell her, "God will tell you whether or not to leave him." But that just led to more indecision on her part. Sheri told me: "Since God hates divorce, I know He would not 'tell' me to do something He hates. So the choice is mine—it's in my hands, not His. I know He'd still love me if I divorced again, but do I want to do something He hates?"

She told me she was financially independent and not afraid of being alone, but she couldn't handle the stigma of being divorced twice.

"I know we are measured many times by our marriage relationship," she said. "It affects how people see us. They don't mean to judge, but I've lived it, so I know. I remember hearing ministers say that if you marry the wrong person, it will mess up your life and potential ministry, and it's true. It's like living in a state of torment, and it affects every area of your life. I don't want my life to be a bad testimony to the church, but unless someone has lived like this, they have no idea what it is like. If I do tell anyone about it, they just tell me to pray, and that's all."

I can only imagine the misery Sheri was going through. I could tell that those same thoughts had been running around and around in her head for years. I've known many other people who have thoughts like that running over and over in their minds, especially the thought that says, "I'm married to the wrong person." Those paralyzing thoughts had tormented Sheri into inaction and caused her untold heartache. My heart went out to her.

Now, I'm no expert on divorce, but I was able to give her some counsel. Because one thing I do know is, the Holy Spirit does lead us in situations like this. There is an answer, and He knows it, no matter how long we've struggled with trying to find one. Our minds can get so bogged down with the same thoughts over and over that making a decision looks hopeless to us. But in Him there really are answers and direction.

Isaiah 43:19 says it this way, "Behold, I will do a new thing; now it shall spring forth; shall you not know it? I will even make a road in the wilderness and rivers in the desert." Even if you've been wandering in the wilderness for years, your Father knows how to make a way out! He can make your life sweet again, with rivers of living water flowing through what has been a dry desert.

There is an answer, and the
Holy Spirit knows it.

We must believe that, especially in a hard situation like Sheri was in. God really does have a plan for each of our lives, and

He also has fresh perspective to help us see current problems in a different light—His light, a new light.

Sheri had been so focused on the "leave or stay" question, but maybe what she needed was a new perspective on her marriage, a new way to treat her husband, a fresh new hope for love and respect to grow between them. Many times if you've been looking so long in one direction, you think there are only one or two answers and you can't see other directions God may want to lead you to. Sometimes a *new* perspective is needed, a brand-new way of seeing the situation. That can come only from time spent with Him.

I know that when the only advice people give us is to "pray," it can sound like a platitude. But then again, as I told Sheri, it really is the place to start. It's the beginning of the answers.

I asked her, "Have you spent concentrated time in prayer and worship lately? Don't even seek God about this particular situation; just soak your spirit in His Word and His love until you can see things the way He sees them."

I also told her to stop beating herself up over her life being a bad testimony to the church. That's just too much pressure for anyone to live up to—and remember where pressure comes from! It comes from the devil, the enemy of our souls, the accuser of the brethren (Rev. 12:10). Don't let him add that kind of pressure on top of your troubles. Yes, we each want our lives to be a good testimony, but that comes from seeking and obeying God, not from trying to be good enough or to do everything correctly in the eyes of others.

And you'll be surprised—when you focus simply on hearing from God and seeing things the way He sees them instead of trying to live up to impossible standards, He'll bring you out on top. Then He'll take what the devil meant for evil and work it for good. (See Genesis 50:20.) He'll bring you through to victory and then use your situation to help someone else. I've seen Him do it again and again.

Sheri clearly needed a new perspective in the midst of her situation, and, remember, sometimes drastic times call for drastic measures. This means that in times like these, a little Word and prayer might not be enough. She needed to step up the dosage and spend *more* time renewing her mind to the Word of God. She needed *more* time listening to the heartbeat of God and letting Him build up her faith. Your answers really can be found in Him, so when you're in trouble or facing major decisions, that's where you should focus your attention on Him.

> When you're stuck in indecision for a long time, you need a new perspective in order to get back on track.

God is the master restorer. He knows how to make all things new (Rev. 21:5). He knows how to make a way where there is no way. And in Sheri's case, a "new way" was needed where there seemed to be no way. Maybe that's true in your case too.

Thankfully she heeded my advice about soaking her spirit in God's Word and prayer. It wasn't long before she reported back to me, "After a few weeks of concentrated time in the Word and prayer—one or two hours every morning—I have received some clear guidance from the Holy Spirit. It's nothing new or revolutionary; He led me back to the basics of forgiveness.

"Although I've walked this painful path many times, and although I thought I had forgiven, He showed me I had not done the complete task. So, I heeded His leading and again went through the process of forgiving my husband and his family."

She went on to say: "Although I don't know the end result

yet, I am freer than I've been in a long time. Abundant peace has returned. Now I am confident that I will not go in the wrong direction, whatever that is. It's a start!"

I'm confident that Sheri will continue seeking the Lord and spending time with Him, and I know He will continue to lead her into the right decisions for her life. She learned a valuable lesson, and I hope we all learned it too after hearing her story. The lesson is, when you're stuck in indecision for a long time, you need a new perspective in order to get back on track. And that comes from spending time with the One who knows the way!

If you're stuck as Sheri was, miserable in the land of indecision, I encourage you to do what she did and bathe your spirit in God's Word through times of prayer and study. He will meet you there, help you get a fresh new perspective, and get you back on track. He'll help you make the right decision. Believe it!

Getting Out of God's Will

Sometimes you may be afraid to make a decision because you're afraid it will be the wrong one and you'll get out of God's will. But listen, if you're earnestly seeking God about the decisions in your life, I believe there are really only two ways to get out of His will. One way is if He has told you to do something—and you *know* beyond a shadow of a doubt He's told you to do it—and you won't do it. That will put you out of His will.

What do I mean by that? Well, suppose God has impressed upon your heart to go to Bible school (or some other kind of school). He's made it clear to you, not once, but multiple times. Yet you don't go. Maybe you have a job or a house or a family or a hundred other reasons why it doesn't make sense to uproot and go to school. You just pass it by every time the idea comes to your mind, saying, "No, I can't do that. I'm not going."

If God is nudging you to go somewhere or do something, it's only for your benefit. If you're resisting Him about it, you're not in His will. I was always surprised by students who came into my office at the Bible school where I was an instructor and said things like, "I don't care what God says, I'm *not* going back to my home church when I graduate from here!" I would say, rather incredulously, "Really? If God is leading you to go back there, isn't it for your own *good*? Do you know more than He does? Are you planning to disobey Him?" Of course they didn't like it when I put it that way, but in essence that's what they were saying.

That's one way you get out of the will of God—by knowing what He wants you to do and not doing it.

The other way to get out of His will is if He has told you *not* to do something—and you *know* He's told you not to do it— but you *want to*, or you don't heed His warning, so you do it anyway. Then you're out of His will too.

Once I heard the story of some missionaries who were staying in a primitive African village, ministering to the natives there. One night as the group was praying, several of the missionaries got a warning in their spirit that they should leave because danger was imminent. Most of the group agreed, and they left, but there were several who said, "No, we won't be chased away—we have authority over that danger, we're people of faith!" So they stayed behind.

Sadly, that very night some evil men raided the village and they killed the missionaries who stayed behind. Afterward some people back home heard about it and said, "Why didn't God protect those missionaries?" Well, He did! But not all the missionaries listened and obeyed. I think many times that is the case when we hear of unfortunate things happening. Very often the Spirit of God was there in advance, warning people, but they didn't listen.

"But I Love Him So Much!"

I also see this scenario when it comes to relationships. A woman will be dating a man, for example, and will say to me, "I don't think he is the one for me. I feel like the Lord is telling me to stop seeing him—but I love him so much!" Or they'll say, "For years I've wanted to be married, and this might be my only chance." Or they may name some other reason for not breaking it off.

I've even had people tell me they can't break up with someone because it would devastate the other person or the other person has threatened to do something drastic if they do. That's all the more reason to run fast and run far from them!

Listen, I understand—no matter who you are, what your age, or how long you've been seeing someone, *breaking up is hard to do* (just as the song says!). But it's not worth hanging on to someone (or something) when the Lord has been nudging you to let them (or it) go. He only wants the best for you. I've seen so many lives ruined by ignoring His leading in this way. And it's really just disobedience. It's *choosing* to get out of God's will.

Now don't get me wrong, God has endless mercy for anyone who has chosen the wrong way in spite of His warning, and He can *still* get them back on track when they turn to Him. But isn't life easier when we listen and obey Him the first time in our decision-making process? Getting out of His will is always painful—for us, and for everyone else involved.

I've seen people do this in other ways too. I knew one woman who wanted a horse more than anything. Her husband didn't, however. They had room to keep one on their property, but her husband had had horses before and knew about the work and expense involved. They didn't have a lot of extra money at that time, and they also weren't home a lot to take on the added daily upkeep of owning a horse.

> It's not worth hanging on to
> someone when the Lord has been
> nudging you to let them go.

But someone offered to give her a horse and she took it, in spite of a feeling in her spirit that she shouldn't, and in spite of the fact her husband didn't want one. She wanted one, bless God, so she stubbornly took it anyway. (Let me just mention here too that she didn't really *ask* the Lord about it—because she knew He'd say no! Oh, that is so dangerous.)

Well, of course the whole situation turned out badly, and in many different ways. Besides daily feeding and exercising (which became a huge burden with their busy schedule), the horse ended up needing a lot of veterinary care, which cost a small fortune. The wife missed a lot of work staying home to meet the vet and care for the horse, which put pressure on her at her job. And the whole thing put terrible financial pressure on their family, as well as her relationship with her husband. She had dishonored him by overriding his wishes, and that stood between them as a constant bone of contention.

What might seem like a blessing can turn out to be a curse if we decide to do something opposite of God's will. That's just called disobedience, plain and simple. And if there's one theme we see over and over in the Bible (both in the Old

Testament and the New Testament), it's that disobeying God never turns out well.

I taught children's ministry for twenty-one years, and I always used to tell kids, "Obedience brings blessing; disobedience brings trouble." It's a pretty simple concept.

Jesus said it this way: "Anyone who hears my teaching and doesn't obey it is foolish, like a person who builds a house on sand" (Matt. 7:26, NLT). We don't want to be foolish! And we don't want to get out of God's will. So let's determine to listen to God and obey Him. Then we'll make the right decisions that lead to blessing in our lives.

> "Obedience brings blessing; disobedience brings trouble." It's a pretty simple concept.

Those are two ways to get *out* of the will of God—disobedient decisions, made on purpose, in direct opposition to the Lord's leading.

Everything else is just a matter of your seeking Him, listening for His voice, endeavoring to hear and obey Him, and walking out what He tells you to do. God can do anything with a heart that says, "Father, I want to obey You. Thank You for leading and guiding me."

Remember what we read in Isaiah 42:16: He's promised to be your guide and help you make decisions every day until you die. Don't be so afraid of making a mistake that you don't make any kind of decision at all. He's got your back. It's going to be OK.

If You've Made a Wrong Decision

What if you've made a wrong decision along the way and now you're stuck with it? I meet a lot of people who are living by that old saying, "You made this bed, now you have to lie in it." But I can't find that in the Bible anywhere! Nowhere does God says, "Too bad you made that wrong decision—now you're disqualified; it's over for you." No! In fact I read in Ephesians 2:4 that He is rich in mercy and loves you greatly! He's more than willing to give you another chance.

So what should you do if you've made a wrong decision? Ask God to forgive you and help you get back on track. Now, I know there are those who might say it's not that simple, especially if there are other people involved. Granted, a wrong decision may have set off a chain of events that can't be reversed, and maybe there are a lot of lives, yours included, that have been affected very badly.

But we can't rewrite the past or take back those wrong decisions. Beating ourselves up over it isn't going to change anything, and it's going to hinder us (and probably others) from moving forward. It's also going to make us miserable!

What's done is done—we have to go on from there. The apostle Paul said it this way, "One thing I do, forgetting those things which are behind and reaching forward to those things which are ahead, I press toward the goal for the prize of the upward call of God in Christ Jesus" (Phil. 3:13–14).

Now, Paul had some pretty major things behind him to forget. He made a lot more wrong decisions than you have. For one thing, he had a part in murdering Christians! My guess is that you haven't missed it that badly. So this verse applies to you and your situation. You *can* move forward from a bad decision. Don't beat yourself up over it. Be like Paul and put it behind you.

Yes, it's better to make the right decision the first time, but we humans are far from perfect. *Everyone* has made some wrong decisions. It doesn't matter how many times you fall down; all that matters is how many times you get back up again. All you have to do is get up one more time than you fall down! You're only defeated when you give up.

It might take a while, but you can count on God. He knows exactly how to help you get back on track and put things back together, even if other people were involved. He is the God of the second chance. In fact, I once heard someone say He is the God of *another* chance. That's good news, because sometimes we even mess up the second chance!

> All you have to do is get up one more time than you fall down! You're only defeated when you give up.

God is incredibly patient with us. He is a Father full of grace and mercy. He doesn't disqualify us when we blow it. As I used to tell my students in Bible school, "God has only had humans to work with for His entire career—He's not freaked out over you!"

Psalm 86:15 says, "But you, O Lord, are a God of compassion and mercy, slow to get angry and filled with unfailing love and faithfulness" (NLT). Micah 7:18 says, "Who is a God like You, pardoning iniquity and passing over the transgression of the remnant of His heritage? He does not retain His anger forever, because He delights in mercy."

You're in Good Company

The Bible is full of people who received second chances, and even third and fourth chances. Look at the apostle Peter. He denied Jesus three times (Matt. 26:74–75) but put that behind him and went on to serve God in a powerful ministry. As I mentioned earlier, not very long after he denied Jesus, Peter preached a sermon on the Day of Pentecost that won three thousand people to the Lord (Acts 2:40–41).

Look at Jonah, who refused to obey God's orders to go and preach to the people of Nineveh and ran as fast as he could in the opposite direction (Jon. 1:1–3). It's one of the Bible's most famous stories—his bad decision landed him in the belly of a giant fish (v. 17). But the story didn't end there. Jonah asked God to forgive him, the fish vomited him onto the beach (Jon. 2:10), and he got a second chance to obey. He went and preached to Nineveh, where there was a great revival, and the Bible says, "The people of Nineveh believed" (Jon. 3:5–10).

One of my favorite second-chance Bible stories is about Mark. This young man traveled with the apostle Paul on his first missionary journey, but he let Paul down one time when he left the team in the lurch. He made a bad decision and just took off when they were in Pamphylia (Acts 15:37–38). It made Paul mad enough to fire him. And, in fact, Paul and Barnabas argued over it so vehemently that Barnabas quit Paul's team and took Mark with him for their own missionary journey (vv. 39–40).

But that's not the end of the story. Years later, toward the end of Paul's life, he was writing to Timothy and said, "Only Luke is with me. Get Mark and bring him with you, for he is useful to me for ministry" (2 Tim. 4:11).

Look at that! We don't know exactly what transpired during the years in between, but obviously Paul gave Mark a second

157

chance somewhere along the way. And Mark took it. He must have repented and worked hard, earning his way back into Paul's favor—so much so that at the end of his life Paul declared Mark was *useful* to him. This infers that all was forgiven and Mark had gone on to be a productive minister. All the bad decisions were left behind. Mark got back up, and his bad decisions didn't end up disqualifying him.

How about King David? This is someone the Bible calls "a man after God's own heart" in *both* the Old Testament and the New Testament (1 Sam. 13:14, Acts 13:22). But this is also a man who goofed up big-time. He committed such major sins that almost anyone would have disqualified him as king and booted him out of the lineage of Christ.

First of all, David saw another man's wife, Bathsheba, taking a bath on a rooftop. Instead of turning away as he should have done, he sent for her and slept with her (2 Sam. 11:1). Huge sin number one! And of course, like most sin, David's sin found him out—Bathsheba became pregnant (v. 5).

So first David tried to hide his sin by getting the woman's husband, Uriah the soldier, to come home from battle and sleep with her, so it would look like the baby was his. But Uriah was loyal to his fellow soldiers, and he told David:

> The ark and Israel and Judah are dwelling in tents, and my lord Joab and the servants of my lord are encamped in the open fields. Shall I then go to my house to eat and drink, and to lie with my wife? As you live, and as your soul lives, I will not do this thing.
> —2 Samuel 11:11

David tried this cover-up ploy twice, but no dice—Uriah wouldn't sleep with his wife.

So then David sent a note back with Uriah to his general, Joab, saying: "Set Uriah in the forefront of the hottest battle,

and retreat from him, that he may be struck down and die"
(v. 15). In other words, David gave orders to have Uriah—
a loyal, hardworking husband and soldier who had done
nothing wrong—killed. And that's just what Joab did. Huge
sin number two!

> Forgive yourself and ask God
> to help you move on because
> His grace extends to you.

Now I doubt that you've messed up as badly as King David
did. And the Lord called him on it, exposing the sin to
everyone (2 Sam. 12:5–15). David owned up to it and repented.
And although he did suffer consequences from his actions (his
baby died, and there was strife in his household from that day
forward), he was not removed from the throne or banished
from the lineage of Christ. No, he remained as king until the
end of his life, and to this day he is still revered as the greatest
king of Israel. Jesus is still called "the son of David" and God
still calls David "a man after his own heart," even in the New
Testament.

Talk about getting back on track! All these people are examples of God's grace. If you've made a bad decision (or several),
you're in good company. Forgive yourself and ask God to help
you move on because His grace extends to you, and He wants
you too to get back on track.

It's Not Too Late

One of the devil's favorite lies is to tell you that it's too
late—you've blown it too many times, you've taken too long
to decide, or, whatever the case may be, it's now over for

you; you're off the track for good. But the devil is a liar, of course. The thing about God is that He doesn't change His mind about you. He devises a plan for your life, and then He expects it to come to pass.

Romans 11:29 says, "God's gifts and God's call are under full warranty—never canceled, never rescinded" (THE MESSAGE). Never! He hasn't forgotten about you or changed His mind about you for one moment. His plan for your life is still the same, even if you have goofed up.

I think Moses is one of the best examples of this. In the Book of Exodus God called Moses to be the redeemer of Israel—to rescue His people, the Hebrews, from four hundred years of slavery in Egypt and deliver them back to the Promised Land. But one day early on, before it was time to put God's plan into motion, Moses was so zealous for his calling and his people that he took matters into his own hands. He murdered an Egyptian who was beating a Hebrew. As a result, Moses had to run for his life (Exod. 2:11–15).

He spent the next forty years as a fugitive in exile, living on the back side of the desert. He married the daughter of a Midianite priest and became a shepherd—quite a step down from redeemer. And we can tell from his later encounter with God that Moses saw himself as having blown it. He thought it was too late and that all he'd ever be from then on was a shepherd.

When God appeared to him in a burning bush and said, "Now's the time to execute the plan, Moses—let's go bring My people out of Egypt," Moses answered, "Who am I that I should go to Pharaoh, and that I should bring the children of Israel out of Egypt?" (Exod. 3:10–11). Clearly Moses believed the devil's lie that it was over for him, that he was a shepherd forever, not a redeemer anymore.

But God was not at all moved by Moses's reluctance. He had a plan and He was going to carry it out anyway!

You know the rest of the story. Through many signs and wonders Moses did go confront Pharaoh, and he was the man who led God's people out of Egyptian slavery. Why? Because God doesn't change His mind about His plan for our lives. Even if we might think it's too late, He doesn't. He didn't change His mind about Moses, and He hasn't changed His mind about you. He knows exactly how to get you back on track.

Better Than a GPS

God is even better at getting you where you're supposed to be than a GPS or navigation system for your car. If you've ever used a GPS, you know what happens when you take a wrong turn. The helpful voice that's guiding you will say something like, "I'm recalculating your route." And you will be told to turn around or take a different way to get where you wanted to go.

God does that too, only better. I've used a navigation system that got hopelessly confused after I went the wrong way—and then we were lost for sure! I've used one that didn't know a road was closed and had no other suggestions for alternate routes to my destination. A GPS can't always see the "road closed" sign!

There's just nothing better than being in the center of God's will for your life—and decisions are the doorway to getting there.

That never happens with God. He's never confused and knows exactly how to get you to your destination or get you back on course. And He's completely willing to do it when you ask for His help.

That's what this book is about: how to hear Him and make the *right* decisions for your life. It's not always easy. Very often there is a lot of pressure in the midst of making a decision because the enemy fights you so hard when you're headed in the direction God wants you to go. But when you seek God and let Him help you make your decision by obeying His directions, it's so worth it! There's just nothing better than being in the center of God's will for your life—and decisions are the doorway to getting there. When you put the principles in this book to work and follow God's best plan for your life, things will turn out "exceedingly abundantly above all that [you] ask or think" (Eph. 3:20).

REVIEW IN A NUTSHELL

We can only get out of God's will through disobedience. We shouldn't be afraid of making the wrong decision (or worried about having made the wrong one), because God can get us back on track. It's not too late.

NOW ENGAGE

Read and meditate on the scriptures we've looked at. Activate the power of God's Word in your life by speaking these declarations aloud:

> Who is a God like you, pardoning iniquity and passing over transgression for the remnant of His inheritance? He does not retain His anger forever, because He delights in mercy.
>
> —MICAH 7:18

DECLARE: "I won't be afraid of making the wrong decision because even if I do, God is big enough to get me back on track. He loves me! I will trust Him, listen to His voice, and bravely move forward."

❧

> Anyone who hears my teaching and doesn't obey it is foolish, like a person who builds a house on sand.
>
> —MATTHEW 7:26, NLT

DECLARE: "I won't get out of God's will by purposely disobeying Him. When He tells me to do something, I'll trust that He has my best interest at heart and I'll do it. When He tells me not to do something, I will also trust Him, and I won't do it. I want to be in His will!"

∞∞∞

> One thing I do, forgetting those things which are behind
> and reaching forward to those things which are ahead, I
> press toward the goal for the prize of the upward call of
> God in Christ Jesus.
>
> —Philippians 3:13–14

DECLARE: "Everyone has made wrong decisions. When I make one, I won't beat myself up. I will ask God for forgiveness and to help me move on. He is patient and merciful with me. He is the God of many more chances! I will forget the past things that drag me down and reach forward."

∞∞∞

> Now to Him who is able to do exceedingly abundantly
> above all that we ask or think, according to the power
> that works in us.
>
> —Ephesians 3:20

DECLARE: "I will seek God and let Him help me make my decisions. I'll obey His directions, and I *will* follow God's best plan for my life. I expect things to turn out exceedingly, abundantly better than I've even dreamed of!"

KEY #9

IF YOU STILL DON'T KNOW…

SOMETIMES AFTER YOU'VE prayed and sought God about a decision, you might feel like you still don't have any idea what to do. There can be any number of reasons for that. It could be because the time is just not right yet—some other things may need to happen before you step out into God's next direction for your life.

So if you've prayed and followed all the other instructions in this book but still aren't sure what to do, don't do anything yet. I promise, the plan God has for you today will still be the plan He has for you tomorrow. You won't get left behind if you wait.

No matter how much of an urgency you might feel, there's no need to get into a hurry. If you're not sure what to do, then don't make a move yet.

Sit Tight

In John 11 we see where Jesus Himself didn't get into a hurry—even when His friend Lazarus got so sick that it was apparent he was going to die. In verse 3 Mary and Martha (Lazarus's sisters) sent for Jesus, saying, "Lord, behold, he whom You love is sick." But Jesus answered, "This sickness is not unto death, but for the glory of God, that the Son of God may be glorified through it" (v. 4). And He stayed *two more days* right where He was! He sat tight.

If you still aren't sure what to
do, don't do anything yet.

Yes, there are times when we have to move quickly if the Holy Spirit prompts us. But in most cases, moving slowly won't hurt anything. I'm sure Jesus's disciples wondered why He didn't get up and go right away to the bedside of His friend. But Jesus didn't let time dictate His actions. He waited for the clear go-ahead from His Father, just as we should do.

When Jesus finally did go to see Mary and Martha, He knew Lazarus had died (v. 14). But He didn't even let *that* bother Him! The Bible doesn't say He rushed to Mary and Martha's house in a panic—or that He rushed to the grave site.

No, He simply told Mary, "Your brother will rise again." Meanwhile, some of the people who had come to mourn with Mary and Martha were murmuring about Jesus. They said, "Could not this Man, who opened the eyes of the blind, also have kept this man from dying?" (v. 37).

But Jesus ignored their words and just proceeded to the tomb—where Lazarus had been buried for four days. He had come to raise him from the dead (v. 44). When Jesus followed God's timing and didn't get into a hurry, a spectacular miracle occurred. Raising Lazarus from a sickbed would have been a notable miracle. But you have to admit that raising him from the *grave* made this example of God's power even more amazing! Many times there is a reason that you shouldn't hurry but should instead sit tight until you know for sure you have God's direction.

Preparation Time

You and I live in a time in which we can have almost anything we want *quickly*. But we have to understand that God isn't moved by our schedule. If you don't believe that, just look how long He's been saying that Jesus will return "soon." Apparently God's idea of soon is vastly different from ours. He's just not in a hurry! His timing is perfect.

Many times you simply are not ready for the next step, and He knows it. He *loves* you and wants you to succeed. He doesn't want to throw you into the deep end before you can swim. You might feel like you're ready—ready for ministry, ready for marriage, ready to move away, ready for that new job. But the truth may be, you are *not* ready! You might still need some work—some experience, some refining, some character development, some education. And God knows exactly how to bring you along, how to take out of you what needs to be taken out, how to put into you what needs to be put in so that you will be successful.

I fully believe that's what He did with Joseph, who had to spend time in a pit, as a slave, and in prison before he could be exalted to his position as second in command over all Egypt. (See Genesis 37–50.) I encourage you to read this story in your Bible. God had to teach Joseph so many things before he could step into that position of great influence.

Joseph was a bit cocky in his youth. He needed a few lessons in humility. He also needed to learn some important things he would have to know if he was going to help govern a country— such as how an Egyptian household is run and how criminals think. God gave him all that during his time of preparation.

It wasn't an easy time for Joseph, when he was a slave and then a prisoner, but it was necessary for getting him into the right place from which he could rescue his people from starvation. In Genesis 50:20 Joseph said, "You meant evil against me; but God meant it for good, in order to bring it about as it is this day, to save many people alive." Your preparation time might not be easy either, but it's necessary for all God needs you to do.

You see, preparation time is never wasted time. It's so important to be well prepared before you step into something new. If you're not, you may have to stop, backtrack, and get prepared. Or you might have to scramble, working on-the-fly as you try to make up for a lack of preparation. Worse yet, you could simply fail at whatever you're attempting because you weren't well equipped.

One thing I've learned over the years is that things almost always take longer than we think they should. Sometimes you will get a glimpse of what God has called you to do or be. Sometimes He'll talk with you about the things He has in store for you. Those things might happen right away—or they might not. It's not really up to you to make them happen according to your timetable. It's just up to you to be ready.

Preparation time is never wasted time.

One minister said it this way: "Sharpen your ax!" If you're going out to chop wood with a dull ax, it will take much longer and you will put in a lot more effort than you would have had your ax been sharp. It's very inefficient to chop wood with a dull ax. But if your ax is sharpened before you go out, then you'll get your chopping done quicker, easier, and with less effort. That's what preparation time is—it's sharpening your ax!

If you're in a season of preparation, I encourage you to embrace it with all your heart. Do you need more schooling? More practice getting along with or submitting to others? More experience in your given field? Sharpen your ax! Don't fight God's timing. Trust Him. Do what He's set before you, and keep your joy. It's far better to move too slowly than to move too quickly and find yourself in trouble. As my spiritual father used to say, "It's easier to play catch-up than cleanup."

Be Faithful

God's method of promotion is and always has been faithfulness. He's looking for people who can be trusted to stick with it through hard times, with a humble, teachable attitude. He's looking for people who will get the job done and not quit in the middle of it. More than talent, charisma, or good looks, God is looking for faithfulness.

So if you've been seeking God about a certain decision and you just aren't getting a definite direction in your spirit, be faithful where you are until you know for sure. Put your hand to something in your local church or in service to God and do it with all your heart. Be faithful on your job and with your friends and family. Let Him see your faithfulness. I heard one minister say it this way, "When God comes to find you (for the next thing He has for you to do), let Him find you busy." God isn't going to promote lazy people.

Matthew 25:23 says that when you are faithful in small things, God will make you ruler over bigger things. You can't expect Him to promote you to the next level in your life until you've proved yourself at the level you're on now. Have you done what He's asked you to do? Have you proven yourself in your current season? And with a good attitude? If not, there's a chance He'll leave you right there until you've gotten this truth and lived it.

You see, God has every right to test you. He did it with Abraham, the original covenant man. In Genesis 22:1 the Bible says, "Now it came to pass after these things that God *tested* Abraham" (emphasis added). God asked Abraham to sacrifice his only son, Isaac. And to his credit, Abraham was completely willing to do it, believing God's Word so much that he concluded "God was able to raise [Isaac] up, even from the dead, from which he also received him in a figurative sense" (Heb. 11:19).

Most of us don't like to hear about being tested. But you might need to change the way you think about it. Really, tests are not a plot and conspiracy against you. A test is to prove what you know, to see if you're ready for the next level. It's sort of like being tested in school. Your math teacher gave you a test from chapter 4 to see if you could do the equations, because if you couldn't, then you weren't ready yet for chapter 5!

Be faithful right where you are,
then you'll be in position for God
to lead you to the next level.

God loves you. He isn't going to throw you into a situation you're not ready for. And He needs to find out if you'll be faithful. How does He do that? You guessed it: He tests you. He wants to see what's in you, to see if you're ready for the next thing and if you'll stick with it. Remember, He's looking for faithfulness.

So my advice to you is, pass your test! Instead of whining and feeling sorry for yourself when going through a test, have a good attitude like the one Abraham had. Put your shoulders back, set your face like flint, and say, "Lord, help me pass my test!" Be faithful right where you are, and then you'll be in position for God to lead you to the next level.

Enjoy the Journey

If you don't know what to do and you're in a season of preparation or waiting, I encourage you to get the most out of the time that you can. And I encourage you to enjoy your current season. It won't last forever, so don't be impatient.

Too many times we set our sights on a goal for our lives, and we push, push, push until we get there, without enjoying the journey. Sometimes we even put off being happy. We say things like: "I'll be happy when...I'm getting paid for ministry; I marry the man/woman of my dreams; I get the perfect job; I've built my dream house; or [insert your own phrase here]."

It's OK to have goals and do everything you can to reach them, but remember to enjoy life along the way. Because on the day you reach that goal, then what? What if you find out reaching that goal *wasn't* the end-all and be-all of happiness? It's so important that you enjoy every phase of your life and every step of your journey.

I promise you, when you reach your goal, you'll still need to use your faith. When you get into ministry, there will be challenges. When you get married, you'll have to *live* with that spouse every day for the rest of your life. When you're working that perfect job, there will aspects of it that you don't like. When you have that dream house, it will need maintenance, or you'll have to replace the roof, or the basement might flood.

That's just life. Don't put off happiness. Don't reserve it for some time in the future.

~~~~~~

It's OK to have goals and do everything
you can to reach them, but remember
to enjoy life along the way.

~~~~~~

If you're in the midst of preparation, give it all you have and enjoy it! There will never be another time like this in your life. If you're waiting on the Lord for your next step, realize that He is working on your behalf even now. Keep your joy, keep your focus on Him, and enjoy every day along the way. Jesus said it this way, "I came that [you] may have *and enjoy* life" (John 10:10, AMP, emphasis added). It's His will for you to enjoy your life, so determine to do it.

REVIEW IN A NUTSHELL

If we don't know what to do, we shouldn't do anything yet. We should sit tight, endeavor to prepare, be faithful, and enjoy every day of the journey.

NOW ENGAGE

Read and meditate on the scriptures we've looked at. Activate the power of God's Word in your life by speaking these declarations aloud:

> Now Jesus loved Martha and her sister and Lazarus. So, when He heard that he was sick, He stayed two more days in the place where He was.
>
> —JOHN 11:5–6

DECLARE: "If I've prayed and applied the keys in this book but I'm still not sure what to do, I won't do anything yet. As Jesus did, I'll sit tight and wait for the clear go-ahead from God. The plan God has for me today will still be His plan for me tomorrow. I won't get left behind. I won't get into a hurry either, because it's easier to play catch-up than cleanup."

⁓∞⁓

> You meant evil against me; but God meant it for good, in order to bring it about as it is this day, to save many people alive.
>
> —GENESIS 50:20

DECLARE: "Preparation time is never wasted time. God loves me and He wants me to succeed, so He won't put His plan into place until I'm ready. I trust Him to take out of me what needs to be taken out and to put into me what needs to be put in. I will spend this time sharpening my ax and I will give it my all."

Well done, good and faithful servant; you have been faithful over a few things, I will make you ruler over many things.

—Matthew 25:23

DECLARE: "God's method of promotion is, and always has been, faithfulness. He's looking to see if I can be trusted to stick with it through hard times, with a humble, teachable attitude. So I will be faithful where I am. I'll be faithful on my job and with my friends and family. I will put my hand to something in service to God and do it with all my heart."

Now it came to pass after these things that God tested Abraham.

—Genesis 22:1

DECLARE: "God has every right to test me, to see what's in me and if I'm ready for the next thing. Lord, help me pass my test!"

I came that [you] may have and enjoy life.

—John 10:10, AMP

DECLARE: "I am determined to enjoy every season of my life. I won't put off happiness. There will never be another time like this in my life, so I will get the most out of it that I can. God is working on my behalf even now, so I'll keep my joy, I'll keep my focus on Him, I'll stay faithful, and I'll enjoy every day along the way."

FEED YOUR FAITH AND STARVE YOUR DOUBT!

PREPARATION TIME OR a season of waiting can be hard on your flesh. So can making a decision and then walking it out. Following through with your decision usually means change is involved, and change can be unsettling, even if you're going in the right direction. It's easy to second-guess yourself or to feel uneasy or impatient when things don't fall together the exact way you expected.

> It's going to take faith to prepare, to
> wait, or to see your decision through.

Notice I said "when" things don't fall together the way you expected, not "if." Because let's face it, nothing is going to happen exactly the way we imagine it will. Just come to grips with that fact and decide to stay in faith!

It's going to take faith to prepare, to wait, or to see your decision through. After you've put the other principles in this book to work and you've made a decision, stick with it. God hasn't brought you this far to leave you—He's going to see you all the way through. So don't waste time second-guessing yourself. Refuse to doubt!

Doubt is the opposite of faith, and 1 John 5:4 says that your *faith* is what overcomes the troubles and trials of this world. When it comes to making the right decision every time, you need faith. You need to keep believing God.

What We Did

When I was moving from Boise to Tulsa, turning my church over to my associate pastor and his wife, I knew we were moving in the right direction, but there were aspects about it that were hard for all of us.

My sons and I had to leave everything behind and strike out on a new adventure. That can be scary. Meanwhile my associate pastor and his wife, although excited about taking over the church, had to actually *do* it!

We all knew we'd made the right decision and were going in the right direction. But I also knew there would be days along the way when the flesh would rise up and we'd all have second thoughts. I knew I'd think, "They get to keep what I poured my life into for almost ten years, and I have to leave!" And I knew they'd think, "She gets to go off to a new adventure, and we're stuck here with this responsibility!"

> After you've made a decision, it's so important to keep your faith built up.

In other words, in walking out this decision there would be temptations on both sides to think or act in the flesh. The same will probably be true for you too. Decision-making time is a crucial time of faith, especially after you've made your decision.

Our solution was to take Communion, reminding ourselves we'd made this decision together and that our relationship was more important than all the feelings going on inside us. Communion sealed the deal between us, and with God. It was a step of faith we took together so we wouldn't be driven by doubts. With that action we vowed to keep our *faith* working during this process instead of letting the occasional uneasiness of the flesh win the day. After you've made a decision, it's so important to keep your faith built up.

Don't Look Back

I once knew a young man who faced a decision about switching jobs. He loved the job he had, but the new job offered exciting new career possibilities and a great deal more money. So he sought God and eventually felt led to take the new job. And it went fine, even though there were things about the new job that he didn't like, of course, just as there are with any job.

After a while, though, he started thinking about how much he liked his other job, and he began to wish that he hadn't taken the new position. At the same time, some difficult things began to happen in his personal life. As a result, he began to doubt his original decision to change jobs, almost as if none of those things would have happened if he'd kept the other job. When he started doubting, he spent all his time looking backward.

While it's OK to reflect on decisions and even change them if you think you made the wrong one, it's not OK to spend all your time looking back and second-guessing yourself. That will just lead to misery—for you and everyone around you.

Don't spend all your time wishing you had done things

differently. Anyone can look at their current situation and want to be someone else, or somewhere else. That is discontentment, and it's largely a choice you make. Learn instead to be content. In 1 Timothy 6:6 Paul says, "Now godliness with contentment is great gain," and in Philippians 4:11, "I have learned in whatever state I am, to be content." Don't let discontentment steal your victory or make you miserable.

Don't let doubt rob you of your victory.

After you've made a decision, do everything you can to move forward and to be content in your situation. Stay in the Word and trust God to tell you if you need to change, but otherwise keep going in the direction you need to go. Don't look back or wish for a different outcome. This is where you are now, so keep trusting God to move forward.

You know the old saying, "You can't drive forward looking in the rearview mirror." It's true. If we carry that analogy even further, we could say, "If you try it, you'll crash!" The same is true in life. It takes faith to keep walking out a decision you've made, and sometimes success takes time. Don't let doubt rob you of your victory.

What God Says About Doubt

The Book of James says: "He who doubts is like a wave of the sea driven and tossed by the wind. For let not that man suppose that he will receive anything from the Lord; he is a double-minded man, unstable in all his ways" (James 1:6–8).

From that verse we can infer that those who single-mindedly stay in faith are *stable* in all their ways. That's how I want to be, don't you? When I ask God for direction, I want to keep my faith on that request and not waver. I want to believe that He is guiding me, no matter what I see or feel. Then once I make a decision, I want to stay in faith about it to keep walking it out without regret.

Decision-making time is a crucial time of faith. But I think that sometimes we feel as if doubting God is an option. Or at the very least, we feel like we can't help doubting. Maybe we think, "I know I asked God to help me make this decision, but now everything's going wrong and I have no idea what to do. Anyone would doubt in this situation, right? It's understandable."

But God doesn't look at doubt like that. He has a very strong opinion about it. In Hebrews 3:7–12 the Bible recounts how the children of Israel didn't get to enter the Promised Land because they doubted God. It uses some very strong language. God calls their doubt "an evil heart of unbelief" (v. 12). He refers to that time in Israel's history as "the rebellion" (v. 8), or what the King James Version calls "the provocation," meaning a period when Israel provoked God—with disastrous results.

Now I don't know about you, but I don't want to provoke God! But that's what the children of Israel did, because they *wouldn't believe.* They wouldn't take God's Word for the fact that the Promised Land belonged to them by covenant right. Instead, they believed more in the giants they saw in the land. And it made God angry.

God was so angry, in fact, that the end result of their doubt was that He denied them entrance into the land. Hebrews 3:19 says, "They could not enter in because of unbelief." The Living Bible says it this way: "And why couldn't they go in? Because they didn't trust him." They doubted God, and it kept them from all the good things He had for them. You don't want to do that!

Notice God didn't say: "Oh, you poor little Israelites, those giants are big, aren't they? I can understand why you doubt My Word and believe more in the giants." No! He wanted them to believe Him! I wonder how many times we believe more in the circumstances (the giants in our life) than we do in God's Word. That's called doubt.

Doubt is believing the devil. It's saying that God isn't big enough to help you or continually guide you. That's essentially what the children of Israel were saying after they sent twelve spies into the Promised Land to spy it out before they entered. (See Numbers 13.)

Some Background to the Story

The children of Israel had been slaves in Egypt for four hundred years when God called Moses to rescue them (Exod. 3:7–9). The entire Book of Exodus tells the story of their miraculous deliverance from slavery and their journey toward Canaan, the Promised Land, as God performed many signs and wonders and miracles on their behalf.

> Doubt is believing the devil. It's saying that God isn't big enough to help you or continually guide you.

Just as they were poised to cross the Jordan River from Canaan, God told them to send over one man from each tribe to spy out the land before they advanced (Num. 13:1). When they did, they found out from the spies that it was a lush and prosperous land. We know that the fruit was huge and luscious, because verse 23 says they brought back one cluster of grapes that had to be carried on poles between two men.

Now, I don't know about you, but the last time I went to the grocery store and bought grapes, I didn't have to take a friend with me to help me carry the cluster home on poles. Those must have been some huge grapes! I picture something the size of beach balls. So, yes, the land was very fruitful, just as God had promised.

That's exactly what the spies said when they returned to give their report to the Israelites. They said, "We went to the land where you sent us. It truly flows with milk and honey, and this is its fruit" (Num. 13:27). But unfortunately the fruit wasn't the only thing these spies had seen in the land. They also saw giants, armies, and fortified cities. They saw that the land was occupied, and they would have to fight for it. So instead of believing God (who had promised them the land in their covenant), they believed in the obstacles:

> Nevertheless the people who dwell in the land are strong; the cities are fortified and very large; moreover we saw the descendants of Anak there. The Amalekites dwell in the land of the South; the Hittites, the Jebusites, and the Amorites dwell in the mountains; and the Canaanites dwell by the sea and along the banks of the Jordan.
>
> —NUMBERS 13:28

Two of the spies, Joshua and Caleb, saw the same giants and the same fortified cities as the other spies, but they chose to believe God. "Then Caleb quieted the people before Moses, and said, 'Let us go up at once and take possession, for we are well able to overcome it'" (v. 30). These two men had the spirit of faith. They believed more in God's promise than they did in the obstacles. They *saw* the obstacles, but they refused to doubt God.

Sadly, the rest of the congregation chose to accept the word of the ten spies who were overcome with fear, and they all began to doubt:

> But the men who had gone up with [Joshua and Caleb] said, "We are not able to go up against the people, for they are stronger than we." And they gave the children of Israel a bad report of the land which they had spied out, saying, "The land through which we have gone as spies is a land that devours its inhabitants, and all the people whom we saw in it are men of great stature. There we saw the giants (the descendants of Anak came from the giants); and we were like grasshoppers in our own sight, and so we were in their sight."
> —NUMBERS 13:31–33

How did they know the inhabitants of the land saw them as grasshoppers? Did they interview them? No. In fact, the inhabitants of the land were afraid of the Israelites! We learn about that forty years later when they eventually do take the land. (See Joshua 2:9; 5:1.) The problem was that the spies saw *themselves* as grasshoppers, and that thought consumed them with fear and doubt, causing them to draw back and miss out on God's promise.

Your circumstances today may be real.
But they're not stronger than God.

This is what happens when we believe what we see and feel more than we believe God. We doubt. We focus on the difficulty, the problem, the giant, the impossibility, the whatever— and it gets bigger than God in our minds. So we become afraid and we side with the circumstances. Doubt cost that generation of Israelites dearly. Because of it, they wandered in the wilderness for forty years and never did get to inherit the Promised Land.

The giants were real. But they weren't stronger than God. Your circumstances today may be real. But they're not stronger than God. Maybe you've made a decision, and now it's getting hard. Maybe you've asked Him for direction and you don't have more ideas than you did before. I can tell you right now that doubt won't get you where you want to go.

Don't doubt God! He just wants you to believe Him. I like what author Kris Mathis says in his blog: "Instead of focusing on what's holding you down, focus on what's holding you up!" It's going to take faith to make right decisions and then walk out God's plan for you.

Feed Your Faith

The only way to stop doubting is to start believing. The only way to starve your doubt is to feed your faith! That is so important, whether you're preparing, waiting, or walking out your decision.

So how do you do that? By giving God's Word first place in your life. By that I mean, give it priority by reading it and meditating on it every day. Also, give it the final say-so in your life. If Israel had kept believing the word of the Lord—to go and take possession of the Promised Land—instead of looking at the giants, they would have taken possession of their land much sooner.

When circumstances say one thing and God's Word says another, side with the Word. Give *it* the final say. For example, perhaps you've made a decision about something, but now things aren't going well. Don't be moved by the circumstances (the giants). Instead determine to hold fast to what God has said in His Word.

Read it every day. Keep encouraging scriptures handy and speak them out when you feel afraid or overwhelmed. If, for example, a doctor says you're going to die, but the Word says by Jesus's stripes you are healed (1 Pet. 2:24), then *choose* to believe the Word over the doctor's report.

It takes faith to make the right decisions—and to stand by them. It also takes faith for seasons of preparation or waiting. Faith comes, according to Romans 10:17, by hearing God's Word. Look every day for God's will in His Word. Decide that if the Bible says it, then you're going to believe it, regardless of the way things look or feel at the time.

That's how to feed your faith. Do it, and you will starve your doubt.

> It takes faith to make the right
> decisions—and to stand by them.

As I said before, you can use the "Now Engage" sections at the end of each chapter as a way to meditate on the Word. Reading the pertinent scriptures and declaring them aloud will help you keep the Word before your eyes and alive in your heart.

Keep the Word before you even when things are going wrong. Refuse to doubt! It takes effort, but you can do it.

REVIEW IN A NUTSHELL

It takes faith to follow through with a decision. Determine to meditate in the Word to keep your faith strong so you can continue walking out your decision without regret or doubt.

NOW ENGAGE

Read and meditate on the scriptures we've looked at. Activate the power of God's Word in your life by speaking these declarations aloud:

> This is the victory that has overcome the world—our faith.
> —1 JOHN 5:4

DECLARE: "I realize that once I make a decision, things will probably not happen exactly the way I expect them to, and it's going to take faith to see my decision through. I'm going to stick with it and keep believing God. I won't be surprised if things become hard on my flesh. God hasn't brought me this far to leave me, so I won't spend time second-guessing myself."

✎✎✎

> He who doubts is like a wave of the sea driven and tossed by the wind. For let not that man suppose that he will receive anything from the Lord; he is a double-minded man, unstable in all his ways.
> —JAMES 1:6–7

DECLARE: "Decision-making time is a crucial time of faith. I determine to single-mindedly stay in faith; therefore I will be *stable* in all my ways. When I ask God for direction, I will keep my faith on that request and not waver, believing that He is guiding me—no matter what I see or feel. Then, after I make the decision, I will stay in faith about it so I can keep walking it out without regret."

~~~

Beware, brethren, lest there be in any of you an evil heart of unbelief.
—Hebrews 3:12

DECLARE: "I don't want to provoke God by doubting. I determine to *believe* His promises and His leading. I will take God's Word for it. I will believe in His promises more than I believe in the 'giants'—the negative circumstances—that may be all around me. I will not allow unbelief to enter my heart and mind."

~~~

They could not enter in because of unbelief.
—Hebrews 3:19

DECLARE: "The children of Israel couldn't go into the Promised Land because they didn't trust God. Not believing God kept them from all the good things He had for them. I won't do that. I will continue in faith, trusting God. Doubt is believing the devil, and I won't do it. I know God is big enough to continue leading me and helping me. I will keep believing Him."

❦

We are not able to go up against the people, for they are stronger than we....We were like grasshoppers in our own sight, and so we were in their sight.

—Numbers 13:31–33

DECLARE: "I will not see myself as a grasshopper in my situation. I will not draw back from this decision because of fear. I will focus on God and His greatness rather than on the difficulty, the problem, the giant, or the impossibility. My circumstances are not stronger than God! I won't doubt Him. Instead of focusing on what's holding me down, I will focus on what's holding me up!"

❦

So then faith comes by hearing, and hearing by the word of God.

—Romans 10:17

DECLARE: "It takes faith to stand by my decision and walk it out. Faith comes by hearing God's Word. So every day I will look to the Bible. I will continually meditate on it. If the Bible says it, then I'm going to believe it, regardless of the way things around me look or feel right now. I will keep the Word before me, even when things are going wrong. That's how I feed my faith. Doing this will starve my doubt."

CONCLUSION

CONGRATULATIONS, YOU'VE MADE it to the end of the book! Hopefully as you arrive here you've learned some things about making decisions. Maybe you've already made one or two decisions in the course of reading this book. Good for you. Now stick with them—and stick with what you've learned about decision making!

The important thing to remember is that God has a good plan for your life, and your decisions are the way that you walk in that plan. He's not hiding the plan from you! That's not what He wants to do. As you seek Him, He will continually lead you into the right decisions for your life.

That's true for today's decisions and tomorrow's decisions as well. You will always be making decisions in your life, so I'm glad you've started learning how to make the right one every time. Just keep going! Whenever you need to, turn to the "Now Engage" sections at the end of each chapter and keep the focus of your faith on God as you make the many decisions of your life and walk them out. May He continue to richly bless you as you follow Him.

YOUR MOST IMPORTANT DECISION

Y OU MAY BE reading this book because you're facing a major decision in your life, yet you realize you've never met the God who holds your future and wants to help you make every decision. I want to invite you into a relationship with Him. Asking Jesus to be your Savior is the most important decision you'll ever make. It's the starting point for getting your life on the right track. You can't understand any of the principles in the Bible, or in this book, until you've started a relationship with Jesus by asking Him into your heart.

There came a time in my life when I had to make a decision to receive Jesus—just as anyone who is a Christian has had to do. I can sincerely say that if it wasn't for Him being in my life, I wouldn't be where I am today. We all are born into sin, according to Romans 3:23: "For everyone has sinned; we all fall short of God's glorious standard" (NLT). Sin separates you, me—everyone—from God.

But two thousand years ago God sent Jesus—His only Son— to the earth as a man to die on the cross and bear the consequences of our sin so we could be restored to a perfect relationship, or "right standing," with God:

> He himself bore our sins in his body on the cross, so that
> we might die to sins and live for righteousness.
> —1 Peter 2:24, niv

Jesus traded places with us—He actually became sin so that we could become righteous in God's eyes:

> God made him who had no sin to be sin for us, so that in
> him we might become the righteousness of God.
> —2 Corinthians 5:21, niv

God loves you, not because you've done everything right or because you're good, but because *He* is good. He loves you so much that He sent Jesus to pay a price for you that you could never pay. He did this because He wants to have a one-on-one, day-by-day, personal relationship with you.

It is God's will for you to be saved. It's the first step in His plan for your life. If you've never received Jesus as your Savior, then you've never received the benefits of what He did for you on the cross. You are still in a sinful state. You're not yet in a position to receive His help for making the decisions of your life.

But you can receive Him *today*. It's not hard.

The Bible says that "if you confess with your mouth the Lord Jesus and believe in your heart that God has raised Him from the dead, you will be saved" (Rom. 10:9). All God's blessings and benefits of salvation can be yours if you receive Him into your heart.

Jesus died for you, but it's your decision—the most important decision of your life—to invite Him into your life.

Think of it like a guy jumping out of a plane with a parachute. Everything goes fine for a while, but unless he makes the decision to pull the rip cord, things are going to turn out badly for him. I encourage you today—pull the cord! You can do it by praying this prayer:

Dear God, I come to You admitting that I am a sinner. I believe that Your Son, Jesus, died on the cross to take away my sin. I also believe He rose from the dead so I can be justified and made righteous through faith in Him. Jesus, I choose to follow You, and I ask that You fill me with the power of the Holy Spirit. Thank You for saving me! Amen.

Congratulations, and welcome to the family of God! If you prayed that prayer for the first time, I'd like to hear from you so I can send you a special gift. Please contact me through my website listed on the "About the Author" page. I also encourage you to get into a good Bible-believing church so you can learn more about your faith and grow in your relationship with God.

BONUS SECTION

AUTHOR Q & A

Get to Know Karen Jensen Salisbury

Q. Tell us a little about yourself.

A. Well, one of my most annoying qualities is that I'm a relentless optimist. I am determined to always see the glass half full! I'm a West Coaster—born and mostly raised in Oregon, although I spent part of my growing up years in California, near the Bay Area.

I was a sports writer in college, and then after I graduated I worked as a TV news writer for a couple years. I love to travel, and these days I'm blessed to travel all over the United States and the world, preaching and teaching at churches, women's conferences, parenting seminars, and other gatherings. Anyone interested in having me come to speak can check out my website at www.karenjensensalisbury.org.

Q. Your first book was published in 2013 and is called, *Why, God, Why: What to Do When Life Doesn't Make Sense.* What is that book about, and why did you write it?

A. It starts out with the story of my first husband dying suddenly in bed at age thirty-seven. We were pastoring a church at the time. He hadn't been sick. He just went to bed and went to heaven. It made no sense—and I had questions! I was asking, "Why, God, why?"

People often ask me how I made it through, how things turned out so well for me and my sons after such a tragedy. Well, it's all in the book. There are so many people who have had terrible things happen to them—not just death, but other kinds of heartbreaking loss and disappointment—and they've gotten stuck there. I wrote *Why, God, Why* to give them permission to ask all their tough questions, then help them move on with their lives and feel real joy again. I like to call it "a handbook for getting past the pain."

My great hope is that it helps people get out of the land of questions and reclaim their lives—to get on with their bright future. Anyone who's gone through a traumatic time can find out more at www.whygodwhybook.com.

Q. What has happened in your life since *Why, God, Why* was released?

A. A lot! I've been privileged to do a lot of radio and TV interviews for the book, which I really enjoy, and to travel and preach its message of hope. And in bigger news, I got married! After seventeen years as a widow, I married a wonderful man from Minnesota in March 2014 and moved to Minneapolis. And, yes, I've heard about the winters there, thank you!

Those who want to see pictures, read the story of how we met, and find out what we've been up to since then, can check it out on the home page of my website, www.karenjensensalisbury.org. Also, right now, as this book is coming out, my first grandbaby is about to be born! I'm so excited to be "Nanna." This has really been a year of increase in my life, and I'm so thankful.

Q. Why did you write this book, *How to Make the Right Decision Every Time*?

A. Everywhere I go, I run into people who are facing decisions in their lives, and they're not sure how to make the right ones. I wanted to help them know that God truly can lead us in every decision. He isn't hiding things from us. He *wants* us to be walking in His divine plan. And when we follow His direction, things can turn out even better than we imagine.

Q. What question are you asked the most?

A. I am asked about writing—how to write a book, where to get inspiration, how to start, how to get published. I've been a writer for most of my life, so when people ask me, "How do you become a writer?" I answer, "You write." Enter writing contests, write in a journal, write for your church, write for your favorite club, write a blog, and write at your job. And if you have a book on your heart, then sit down and write it. There's no magic formula. It takes work. Thomas Edison said that success is 10 percent inspiration and 90 percent perspiration. The same is true for writing! You have to put words on a page. Do it every day. That's what most people won't, can't, or don't do. Writing is mostly hard work. If it were easy, everyone would do it!

As for publishing, I still don't know what advice to give because my relationship with Charisma House came about in a completely supernatural way that doesn't usually happen for most people. But I will say this—I prayed about getting published for years, and it happened—and it can happen for you too. If God has put a book on your heart, then He has a way for you to get it published. So get writing!

Also, remember that publishers need writers. They are always looking for good manuscripts, so don't be afraid to submit yours. Put effort into writing a good book proposal. And for more information on how that's done, just type "how to write a good book proposal" in your search engine.

You can submit a proposal to Charisma House by going to www.charismahouse.com/submit-book-proposal. Another good resource is *Writer's Market: Where and How to Sell What You Write*. Go to www.writersmarket.com.

Q. Tell us something about yourself that very few people know.

A. I play the piano. And I can make a croaking noise just like a frog.

BIBLIOGRAPHY

Kelly, Bob. *Worth Repeating: More than 5000 Classic and Contemporary Quotes*. Grand Rapids, MI: Kregel, 2003. 230.

Martin, Francis P. *Hung by the Tongue*. Lafayette, LA: Francis P. Martin Bible Teaching Seminars, and Tapes, 1979.

Mathis, Kris. "Feed Your Faith and It Will Starve Your Doubts!" Blog. WordPress.com, December 12, 2012.

Merriam-Webster's Collegiate Dictionary. 11th ed. Springfield, MA: Merriam-Webster, 2003.

Strong, James, and Gordon Lindsay. *Strong's Concordance: Bible Dictionary; Study of the Words of Jesus*. Charlotte, NC: P.T.L. Television Network, 1975. 102.

ABOUT **THE** AUTHOR

Karen Jensen Salisbury has been in ministry for about thirty years and a writer for about forty. She and her first husband, Brent, traveled as itinerant ministers and also pioneered two churches in the Northwest.

In 1997, upon Brent's unexpected death, she became senior pastor of their church in Boise, Idaho. She raised their sons, Josh and Ryan, through their teenage years into young men on fire for God.

She was an instructor at Rhema Bible Training College in Broken Arrow, Oklahoma, from 2005 to 2014. In 2014 she married Bob Salisbury, a businessman from Minneapolis. Karen travels and ministers across the United States and overseas, sharing what she has learned about the faithfulness of God through good times and bad.

Her teachings and writings have influenced the lives of hundreds of thousands of people all over the world. Her humor, her never-give-up attitude, her love for God, and her strong stand on His Word will bless and inspire you.

VISIT KAREN'S WEBSITE

KAREN
JENSEN
SALISBURY

GO TO www.karenjensensalisbury.org
WHERE YOU CAN:

- Contact her personally – she'd love to hear from you

- Book her for speaking engagements

- Shop for Mp3s, CDs, DVDs, books, etc.

- Watch videos of Karen

- Read her blogs "Parenting With Faith" and "*This Is the Life*"

- Be encouraged by her archived teachings

- Follow her itinerary

- And more…

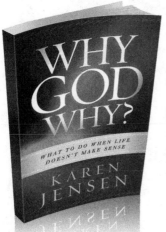

HELP  PARENTS

HOST A PARENTING SEMINAR

Karen has conducted *Parenting With a Purpose Seminars* throughout the U.S. and overseas. Her seminars cover both spiritual and practical aspects of parenting for both married and single parents.

Seminar topics include:
- God's plan for your family
- Surrounding your children with faith and love
- Obedience and correction
- Roles and stages of parenting

"This seminar was far above everything I expected. It has equipped me with information that I needed to properly launch my children into their destinies." **R.T.**

HELP & ADVICE FOR RAISING YOUR KIDS

These powerful and practical Bible-based lessons have helped families around the world, and can equip and encourage any parent, no matter the age of their child.

CDs or DVDs materials for personal or group use:
- 16 half-hour lessons
- Great for personal use or group study (cell groups, church classes, special meetings, community outreach)
- Workbooks and Group Leader workbook available
- 31 Day devotional for parents

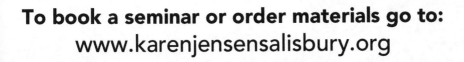

To book a seminar or order materials go to:
www.karenjensensalisbury.org

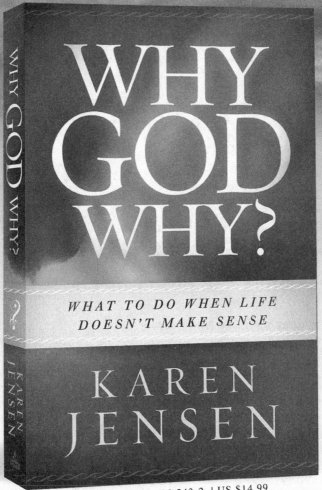